Malaysian Cooking

A Master Cook Reveals Her Best Recipes

by **Carol Selva Rajah**

foreword by **David Thompson**
photography by **Masano Kawana**
styling by **Christina Ong** and **Magdalene Ong**

TUTTLE PUBLISHING
Tokyo • Rutland, Vermont • Singapore

CONTENTS

Tapping Into Delicious Memories

I have been fortunate enough to have eaten Carol's food many times, sometimes with Carol sitting next to me telling me the most marvellous tales of her family, her Amah and her childhood in Malaysia. I sat mesmerised as she wound her stories around her food—until I was not sure which was the more alluring. But I was always left wanting more, and I was not alone in this as I know many who have been held in the same thrall of her charm and her cooking.

"We cooked for pleasure," she told me. "We forgot which community we belonged to and we cooked to feed and to please our friends—whether they were Malays, Chinese, Tamils, or later Australians." And such hospitable charm fills this book.

Malaysian Cooking is an account of these stories and their dishes—a dance through her childhood, tapping into delicious memories with the steady, rhythmic clunk of the granite pestle pounding the spices and filling our senses with the pungent aromas that still hold such a powerful sway over her and her cooking. The garden of her youth was filled with lemongrass, galangal, roseapples and durians. Her Amah's Aromatic Chicken Curry skips straight out of her rich, happy past. I can imagine it served with Fragrant Pandanus Coconut Rice (*Nasi Lemak*), or on special occasions with Lacy Malay Coconut Pancakes (*Roti Jala*). Flaked fish salad with spices and coconut was a dish which her husband, Selva, insisted on preparing himself to ensure the proper seasoning, while her "lethal weapon" of Babi Tayu (*Tau Yew Bak*)—Sweet Soy Pork with Mushrooms and Star Anise—packs an Amah's love!

This book is not just based in the vivid but somewhat distant past. It is a collection of the author's memories throughout her life—and it contains many recipes that are not just Malaysian. They are her own authentic recipes reflecting her life's journey.

Malaysian Cooking evokes more than just memories—it excites the imagination and fills the senses with the possibilities of pungent fragrances and tastes that create new memories. It articulates the past and present of a talented cook in the very best way—with wonderfully delicious recipes!

David Thompson
Winner of the James Beard Award
and IACP Finalist for *Thai Food*

Fragrant Memories from Malaysia

by Carol Selva Rajah

Fragrance evokes memories. If you have ever entered a bread shop while cinnamon buns are baking or passed someone's kitchen at Christmas and whiffed the spicy aromas of a Christmas cake or breathed deeply as you walked through a pine forest after a spring rain, then you will share some of my passion for fragrance in food and its ability to stir up memories of the past. This phenomenon has been most famously described by French author Marcel Proust, as he sipped a cup of tea and ate a soggy madeline biscuit. This simple and almost mundane act of eating and drinking set off a chain reaction of fragrance, awakening long-lost memories and indeed becoming the inspiration for one of the greatest of all literary works—his classic novel, *Remembrance of Things Past (A la recherche du temps perdu)*. Simple, humble tastes and smells have the power to project us back to our childhood and remind us of a forgotten event or moment faster and more effectively than almost anything else; and always remind me of Proust's madeline.

My own childhood, spent in Malaysia and Singapore, abounds with fragrant memories which have inspired the recipes in this book and built up my appreciation for fragrant home-cooking. Walking through the tropical spice gardens of Bali, Penang or Sri Lanka, your senses are overwhelmed by a combination of distinctive aromas as you stop and mentally attempt to separate them into what is culinary and what is purely floral. For me it is like a dance through my childhood and a mental game of guessing the ori-

gins of each aroma. I have found that in Malaysia the ingredients from gardens, kitchens and floral markets overlap as they are all used in cooking, conjuring memories of a mouth-watering curry from a street stall in Chiang Mai or Singapore's Newton Circus. With this book I hope to inspire you to create new "food memories" with simple, deliciously fragrant recipes drawing upon the vast rainbow of aromatic produce one finds in traditional Malaysian kitchens.

When I was growing up in Malaysia, beautiful scents were all around us, pervading our lives. I lived with my family on a large sprawling property planted with a jumble of fruits and herbs. Mango and rambutan trees framed my window, the aroma of mango flowers brushing past the mosquito netting, spreading their light caramel-like fragrance around my room. Now whenever I bite into a juicy Bowen mango from Queensland, I close my eyes and am immediately transported back to the warmth and comfort of my childhood bedroom. Stalwart jackfruit trees stood like soldiers along the back fence, producing meter-long fruits which resembled spiky green

ABOVE: Drawing of the family home and garden in Klang near Kuala Lumpur. To the left of the old colonial bungalow was the attached kitchen with herb garden beds and badminton court. On the right were orchids and various fruit trees. In front of the house stood the bougainvillea bower and the fish pond underneath it (as shown in the diagram). OPPOSITE: My father and mother when they were very young sitting in the garden by the side of the house. By the time I had grown up this garden was filled with rambutan, mango, jambu, roseapple, and jackfruit trees.

balloons hanging ponderously from the stems. As these fruits slowly matured, they gave forth a spicy, pineapple-honey scent that enticed everyone passing the open breezeway to the kitchen and the chilli beds beyond. These beds were only chilli in name—in fact they were littered with the distinct lemon-oil scents of lemongrass and galangal and the pungent, oily turmeric, yielding a tousled jumble of aromatic citrus and rose whenever disturbed, especially on a hot afternoon. These herbs and spices were gathered and tossed together on occasion into a beautifully tart jackfruit salad—colourful, fragrant and deeply satisfying, having come straight from our own garden.

Our garden was a place where you ate with your eyes and your nose before you even got to the dining table. There was perfume everywhere. In front of the house was a high metal planter that supported scarlet bougainvillea and delicate white flowers of orange blossom and red hibiscus which were thrown into juicy Sri Lankan sambols. Under this impressionist splash of colour sat a circular fish pond with darting blue fighting fish, watched benignly by the resident tortoise. Nearby was a mass of blue pea flowers that coloured our Nonya cakes and gave off a delicate perfume. Behind the house, an old roseapple or *jambu ayer* tree struggled for survival, laced with pale lichen and crawling with giant red ants, all headed for the special juicy sweetness in the fruit that we, as children, all craved. These beautiful juicy roseapples had the aroma of peaches and were used in our family *Rojak* salad—their sweetness contrasting with the spice of chilli and pungent shrimp paste.

On one side of the house we had curry leaf bushes which gave off peppery aromas that ended up in my father's hot Ceylonese curries and a famous sour, salty Mulligatawny soup known as *rasam* in India. The subtle, newly-mown grass scent of the pandanus palm pervaded our garden and glamorised our coconut rice

cakes. Father's bud-grafted trees, gnarled and bent with heavy green pomelo fruits, with pink pockets of lemony-sweet fruitiness on the inside, jostled with the lime trees whose fruit was indispensable in the kitchen. Everytime my father was annoyed, my Amah would produce her pomelo and prawn salad to placate him with its soothing colours and aroma, often involving the *jambu ayer* roseapple and several herbs from the garden. The kalamansi lime bushes with their cherry blossoms of dark green that spurted orange-sweet juice that was used for the ubiquitous lime cordials—so loved for their thirst-quenching properties, was a necessity in the tropical heat. Nothing was wasted—the spent fruit, rind and all, was massaged into scalps to create squeaky-clean, lime-perfumed and shampooed hair, again a strong Proustian channel to childhood innocence.

Central to all of this was the kitchen, tucked onto the back of the house yet the pivot of the home. The kitchen was divided into two areas: the "wet-kitchen" where pounding, grinding and slicing of spices and herbs was done each morning in preparation for a meat or fish curry, close to a running tap so that everything could be splashed clean. The other "dry-kitchen" was for cooking—where the old wood and coal stove sat squat across from the sink and wash area, and on it, a huge pot bubbled quietly with a joint of mutton for a curry or filled with chicken bones for stock inside. A vast wok sat on top of the stove almost permanently where a special dry chicken curry would be slowly sautéed, full of potatoes, tomatoes, chilli and plump chicken pieces. I remember being drawn to the kitchen by the sharp, nose-tickling spike of the chilli as it splattered into the hot oil, burning my eyes and nostrils until the onion and the soothing garlic were thrown in and left to mellow slowly in the wok. Amah, my "other mother," would be there, stirring the mixture calmly, adding the soft citrus and gingery aromatics—the lemongrass

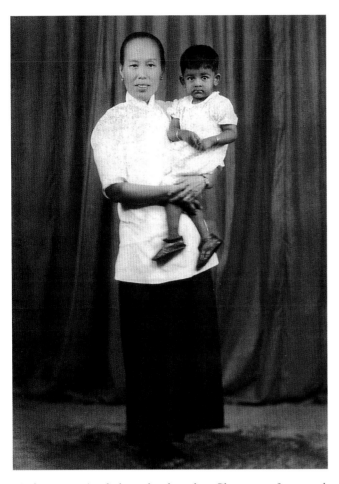

My Cantonese Amah dressed in her white Chinese samfu top and black pyjama pants holding me on my second birthday.

by my mother's colonial associates and missionary friends. These recipes were all eagerly borrowed, recorded and tested again and again at our home until they gradually became our own, carefully recorded in old broken-spined school exercise books.

Every morning before school, under Amah's expert tutelage, I learned to pick and portion the herbs. In one instance lemongrass, galangal, chilli and turmeric would evolve into a mouth-watering curry paste for her unique sambal prawns (page 80). We would start first with a collection of chopped onion and garlic and pounded shrimp paste and tamarind puree. Working on the grinding stone, she would grind the chilli, pulverise the onion and garlic, then add the rock-hard turmeric—so difficult to judge, colouring everything it touches with a saffron stain—until it splinters and releases its rose-musk fragrance. Lemongrass would go in next. As more herbs were added, they actually made the grinding easier. From her I learned the secret of layering ingredients when cooking, adding first the garlic and waiting for it to release its enticing aromas, then adding the next ingredient and then the others in their turn so that the oils and fragrance in each spice was released separately to build on the flavour of what came before. The sambal prawns that finally emerged was a mixture of all these perfumed ingredients and remains an indelible memory of my ancestral home.

While we went to our gardens frequently for the aromatic herbs and spices for the grinding stone, it would be off to the jostling, noisy market for our fresh produce—always at dawn before the sun wilted away the best ones. Crisp green beans and jelly-like tofu—shaking as we picked it up from its aromatic banana leaf container—and the fresh scents of *kailan* (chinese broccoli), and mustardy *choy sum* (flowering cabbage) with its peppery yellow flowers, jewel-like eggplants and bright green, knobbly bitter gourds—all of these would be carefully selected, wrapped and dropped into our bulging shopping basket.

Malaysian markets are tumultuous, exciting places. Some are mere collections of tiny little thatched lean-tos. Others are rambling, colourful and well-stocked. How lavish the brightly-coloured mix of the vegetable stalls always seems. Pyramids of fresh green wing beans—I salivate at the thought of using them for a quick, crispy stir-fry with dried prawns and slowly caramelising onions. Orange and saffron-coloured

and galangal and the earthy, fecund shrimp paste—finally converting it all miraculously into a composite of satisfying aromas, flavours and colours.

Amah was a natural cook, a master of flavour and aromatic patterns. As part of my multicultural extended family, she observed and learned the Jaffna Tamil and Malay influences of our country and added it to her own store of cooking and Chinese herbal lore. She was Cantonese but her and our food heritage was from everywhere. Sri Lankan fish and shrimp curries with their soul-satisfying coconut soupy sauces followed the spicing rules of my father's people. For Chinese cuisine, we adhered to the strong herbal and saucing traditions of Amah, intertwined with my mother's early Hokkien and Nonya food experiences in Penang, where her first loves were the hot and spicy shrimp pastes and chilli heat of the Nonya Laksa and Mee Siam. There were other influences of course, like the Malay dishes that friends and neighbours prepared and the formal European dinners that were given

Shopping for aromatic herbs and vegetables in Sydney's Asian market at Cabramatta, where the largest concentration of Asian migrants live, grow their market produce and serve an amazingly eclectic range of Asian foods.

bananas, bright red tomatoes, towers of food looking so neat yet so precarious. What hilarity to see them accidentally scattered amongst the regal purple brinjals (eggplants) and the jungle-green bittersweet drumstick beans! The sweet fragrance of coconut, reminiscent of ripe cucumber, cream and pandan is a Proustian link to palm trees and beaches, so familiar to us all, and a unifying element amongst all the wonderful countries and cuisines of the tropics.

Markets smell different in Asia than elsewhere. Enter one and you are met with an onslaught of fragrances: musky, fishy, yeasty, nutty. The salty tang of fresh fish in large, musty-wet bamboo baskets—I picked up some whiting so fresh it almost leapt at me! The trevally is particularly tempting and the snapper always inviting because of its pink shiny scales. Further down, there are the caramel-like smells of roasting chicken satay. The pungency of chilli powder being ground; the clean aromas of galangal and warm nutmeg; the sweet scent of cardamom and cassia perfumed

tea, poured out in a tall, thin stream to create a magnificent, spicy froth. Asian markets are always a beehive of activity with people jostling and carrying baskets—busy, busy everywhere.

Aromas alone can announce the culture and the nationality of a market. Indian markets are suffused strongly with the pungency of curry leaves, cumin and coriander. The magical dry-roasting of these spices creates completely new aromas, such as those found in a vegetarian dhal dish cooked with tomato and garnished with black mustard seeds and frying onions. And everywhere in India there is the faint lingering aroma of cardamom and chocolaty cinnamon.

Chinese markets announce their presence by the squawking of live ducks and chickens and row upon row of pork butchers. Herbal concoctions boil in vats and onion-mustardy smells emanate from rows of stalls selling *choy sum*, bok choy, *een choi* and various other cabbages piled in pyramids with other greens. In another area one finds assorted pickles and preserves

11

in large earthenware jars, close to stalls with charcoal braziers where pork is slowly roasted, yielding the arresting sweetness of *hoisin*, and the ever-enticing caramel aromas of *char siew* pork and anise-glazed ducks which hang on hooks like soldiers in a row.

Every country has its characteristic aromas: the Balinese ones are best represented by the delicately perfumed ginger flower chopped into the *babi guling* roast pork salad; Thailand by its coriander and lemongrass with peppery chilli and the lemony tang of its Tom Yam Soup and Mee Krob; Vietnam by the herbal fragrance of perilla in its beefy Pho soups.

The importance of aroma

Over three quarters of what we taste in fact comes from smell. When we put food in our mouth, its aromas travel to the back of our throat and up to the nose. To demonstrate this to my students, I have them eat a few grains of strong, aromatic cumin, fennel and sugar while their nose is blocked with a clothes pin. They get nothing—no sensation of taste or smell. Then I have them remove the clothes pin. Whoa! Smell and taste return with surprising force.

Max Lake, the famous food and wine critic and my personal mentor and friend, has reinforced and influenced a great deal of my own understanding of aroma and taste. He writes that olfactory memories are strong because the nose is connected to the primitive brain, and thus connected to our sensual drives. Perfumers and sommeliers have long been aware of this relationship. His analysis of how the part of the brain devoted to smells affects our enjoyment of food and wine serves to confirm what I have learned through personal experience—that the emotional and physical functions of the brain are conjoined via the nose.

Because they are so closely tied to personal and cultural memories, aromas affect different people in very different ways. The smells of a ripe durian and of a ripe blue cheese are equally strong, yet they evoke either repulsion or greedy anticipation in a person depending upon whether their upbringing is Asian or Western. However, a look at the long queues at a bread shop or an Italian pizza shop redolent with roasting garlic, will also confirm that many aromas are universal.

I feel that taste memory—the ability to perceive and differentiate between aromas—is always present in a

ABOVE: Elegant star anise pods—an aromatic star-shaped spice with the fragrance of cassia and anise. OPPOSITE: Fresh garlic chives not only look attractive, they pack a garlic punch when added to a tossed noodle dish or a chilli crab dish (see Chilli Crabs with Ginger and Garlic Chives—page 78).

person, but requires training through cultivation and practice. I recall Amah's natural ability to use her taste and smell memory to recreate flavours in a dish quite foreign to her. Once she tasted something, her own senses would guide her through a personal library of ingredients and formulae, enabling her to cook from intuition rather than from a written recipe. Even if the ingredients were not quite right, as when she tried a new curry recipe (she was not Indian, but Cantonese), she managed to arrive at the desired flavour anyway by adding other ingredients—for example a thick soy sauce. Friends often wondered why Amah's curry had such powerful flavours. This ability to recreate flavours from memory is one of the most desirable gifts that all good chefs the world over possess.

This leads me to the concept of *yin* and *yang*. Another attribute of Malaysian cooks is the ability to achieve a balance in their cuisine between the opposing energies of *yin* (earth, darkness, cold and receptivity) and

ABOVE: Pickled garlic can be truly surprising when used in salads and meat dishes and can be easily made at home.
OPPOSITE: Perfect for a summer lunch that speaks of rarefied paradise (see Black Pepper Lobster Tails with Garlic Butter—page 82) with a glass of your favourite bubbly.

yang (sunlight, heat and activity). In food this is important because some foods are known to be cooling (*yin*) and others heating (*yang*). This relationship is encouraged and fostered in both aroma and flavour, and has little to do with actual temperature, but more with creating heating and cooling sensations in the body with dishes and their ingredients.

Yin aromas have a calming effect on the *chi* (life force or human energy). Examples of this are the delicate, almost feminine perfumes of the grassy pandanus and green teas, the citrusy lemongrass, the floral bouquets of the ginger flower or the delicate *keng hua* (cactus flower). *Yang* aromas are warm and stimulating. Examples are pepper, ginger, chilli and the musky and nutty aromas of spices and some meats. Do not turn down a cup of "heaty" ginger tea offered to you when you have a cold coming on—the aromas will clear the sinuses and the ginger will warm your chest.

I have often felt homesick for the tastes and smells

and that little chilli patch back home, and for the Malaysian kitchens which always beckon with their spicy, intriguing aromas that change each day as the daily menu changes. Living in Australia, I slowly came to realise that in the West herbs are subtle and gentle, whereas the herbs used by Malaysians are intense and fiery, and clash together as they cook in the wok. Moreover, the spices that are strong in their own right, such as cumin, coriander and fennel, are often dry-roasted to give them added punch. This represents a major difference in our cultures. Our cuisine in the East is so aromatic because that is what is most important to us. Good Malaysian cooks are trained to bring out the aromas of each individual spice or herb. Garlic aromas are teased out in woks, and curry pastes are slowly cooked until they became aromatic. The abundance of perfumed ingredients makes it easy to create such food once you understand this simple point. To this day I live by one of my Amah's major tenets: *"Ahh, ho heong, ho sek mah!"* which means "Good smell, good to eat!"

Friends who travel with me to Malaysia are enraptured. One friend, a television producer, used to looking at things through the confining lens of a camera, turned to me in the midst of filming a market and remarked that he wished he had a "smell-a-vision" camera. Canadian and Australian friends repeatedly walk into my kitchen and are seduced by the aromas, immediately heading for the stove and lifting up the lids to breathe deeply of their contents, trying to analyse each of the dozen herbs and spices I had painstakingly layered into a tender rich Rendang. An Australian diplomat who had lived in Asia for many years once walked into my home and immediately asked whether I had forgotten he was coming to dinner. Prior to his arrival, I had cleaned the kitchen thoroughly and sprayed it with air freshener to extinguish the curry smells and he assumed there was nothing cooking! I never did that again. Today I bask in the aromas of my food and its glorious flavours, and my kitchen remains a proud outpost of my native land.

This book was born from a discovery that Malaysian flavours and aromas are simple to recreate in your kitchen. Follow my Amah's rule "If it doesn't smell good, it will not taste good!" Just go ahead and have fun with these recipes.

Essential Malaysian Ingredients

Asian eggplants are generally smaller than Mediterranean eggplants. Some are long and cucumber-shaped or ovoid, while others are about 4 cm (1¹/₂ in) thick and boomerang-shaped with a regal purple colour. They come in a variety of shades of purple, mottled purple or green, and distinctive among them is the bright green pea eggplant which has a peppery centre and is often used by the Thais in green curries. The eggplant is used in curries, pickles, sambals or mashed rather like the Baba Ganoush of the Middle East.

Banana leaf This is commonly used to cover or wrap foods in Asia. It has a light grassy and wax-like aroma that transfers to any food cooked in it. In Malaysian homes, banana leaf is a sensual steaming wrapper for rice, fish or meat smeared with some lemongrass, garlic and other herbs. Banana leaves are obtainable from Asian markets. Look for the leaves wrapped in large bundles. They are usually sold by weight, with the thick centre ribs removed and the leaf portions folded. A good substitute for wrapping purposes is lotus leaf or aluminium foil.

Bok choy is a highly nutritious variety of cabbage with long, crisp stalks and spinach-like leaves. It has a clean, slightly peppery flavour and is a wonderful addition to soups and stir-fries. It is available in most well-stocked supermarkets.

Brown bean paste The basic brown bean paste is fermented from sweeter yellow soybeans which are less intense and have a maltier flavour. The best brown bean paste is a golden toffee-coloured paste, with an earthy mushroom and yeasty aroma. Look for them in the condiment section of Asian markets. Mash whole beans with the back of the spoon before adding it to the dish. Hoisin sauce may be substituted.

Asian shallots are small, round and pinkish-purple and add a sweet, oniony flavour and a hint of garlic to countless dishes. They are sliced, deep-fried and used as a garnish. Asian shallots are smaller and milder than those found in Western countries, with less juice so that they fry more easily. French shallots may be substituted, but use only half to a third as many as the recipe calls for as they are much larger.

Betel leaves They are the spicy and highly nutritious leaves from a vine that is related to the pepper plant. There are two varieties of the betel leaf, both growing on climbing vines. The Thai and Vietnamese variety, used to wrap finger foods, is called *chaplu* and is less bitter and softer than the tougher variety chewed with betel nuts and calcified lime. Grape leaves are a good substitute.

Cardamom Originates from India, this spice is available as dried pods or in ground form. Cardamom pods are generally green but are also available in bleached white pod form. There are three ways of using cardamom: as whole pods, as whole seeds or by grinding the seeds to a fine powder. Lightly crack open the whole pods before using. If using the seeds, peel the pod to extract the small, dark seeds inside and then grind them in a mortar. Substitute equal parts of ground nutmeg and cloves or cloves and cinnamon.

Dried red chillies

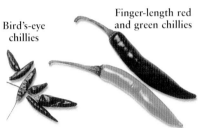

Bird's-eye chillies

Finger-length red and green chillies

Chillies Many different varieties of chillies are used in Malaysia. The flavour of fresh and dried chillies is different, so be sure to use the type specified in the recipes. Finger-length green and red chillies are usually moderately hot. Red chillies are often dried and ground to make chilli flakes and ground red pepper. Tiny but fiery-hot bird's-eye chillies may be red, green or yellow-orange. Cut or break dried chillies into pieces and soak them in hot water for about 10 minutes to soften them before grinding or blending. If you want to reduce the heat without losing the flavour, discard some or all of the seeds.

Chinese black vinegar This is very similar in colour and aroma to the Italian balsamic vinegars, except there is a slight overriding aroma of soy and five spice powder, where the western vinegars have more wine aromas. If unavailable, substitute balsamic vinegar, although the flavours and aromas will be slightly different.

Chinese broccoli Also known as *kailan* or Chinese kale, Chinese broccoli has long, narrow stems and leaves, and small edible flowers. The stems are the tastiest part of the plant while the leaves are slightly bitter and are often discarded. Chinese broccoli is available fresh in all Asian markets and many supermarkets. Substitute broccoli stems, bok choy or broccolini.

Chinese pickled mustard greens Also known as *kiam chye* or *xian cai*, this is a slightly sour and extremely salty brined vegetable. Soak it in fresh water for at least 15 minutes to remove some of the saltiness, repeating if necessary. It is available in vacuum packs from well-stocked Asian supermarkets.

Cinnamon and cassia Both cinnamon and cassia are commonly sold in sticks or in powdered form. True cinnamon can be distinguished from cassia by its lighter colour and finer powder. Always buy just the quantity you need as this spice loses its fragrance quickly. Substitute nutmeg or allspice.

Cloves With a unique shape that resembles a small nail, the clove is actually the unopened flower bud of an attractive tropical tree—the buds are picked before they flower and sun-dried to a brownish black. It is warm, pungent, peppery and numbing in flavour and has a very strong aroma that is a mix of cardamon and camphor. Cloves are sold whole or in powdered form in Asian markets. This is a spice that can easily overpower a dish, so always use it sparingly. Allspice can be used in place of ground cloves.

Coriander leaves The coriander leaf has the most complex of herb flavours: it is spicy, citrusy with hints of lime, and almost pungent and curry-like, all at the same time. All parts of the coriander plant are used. Fresh leaves are often chopped and added to salads and fillings in Malaysian cuisines, the seeds are used in curry pastes, and the pungent roots are mainly ground into Thai curries. Dried coriander leaves do not have the wonderful flavour and aroma of fresh ones, although they can be used.

Coriander seeds These are the small round beige seeds of the coriander plant. They have a distinct lemony aroma with back notes of musk. These seeds, when dry-roasted and ground, are the main flavouring ingredient in Malaysian curries as the mild flavour adds balance to other more strongly-scented spices like cardamom and nutmeg. Coriander seeds are available whole or ground in Asian food stores. Coriander seeds can be used in three strengths—when a mild flavour is required, add them whole or sauté them with other spices. For a more pronounced, lemon–aniseed flavour, grind the seeds and add them to curries. For a particularly intense flavour, dry-roast the seeds in a pan until fragrant, cool and grind them to a powder. Substitute equal parts of fennel and cumin with a pinch of turmeric.

Cumin Closely resembling caraway or fennel seed in appearance, cumin is lighter and slightly larger than caraway but smaller and narrower than fennel. Dried cumin seeds are elongated, almost like the hull of a boat, hairy and brownish in colour with a striped pattern containing nine ridges and a tiny stalk attached to the end. Whole and ground cumin are widely available in supermarkets or Asian food stores. Substitute fennel or aniseed.

Coconut cream and coconut water

Freshly grated coconut

Coconut milk

Coconut and coconut milk Nowadays canned, bottled or packet coconut milk or cream are readily available in the Asian food sections of most supermarkets. These vary widely in consistency and flavour, depending on the brand, and you will need to try them out and adjust the consistency by adding water as needed. Coconut milk is a common ingredient used in most Malaysian cuisines, notably as a base for curries. Coconut cream is the creamy liquid extracted from the first pressing of the grated coconut flesh. It is mainly used to make desserts and rich curries. Coconut milk is obtained from the second and third pressings. If coconut milk is not available, use powdered coconut milk or fresh milk or cream. Packets of dried or freshly grated coconut, sweetened or unsweetened, are also available in the baking sections of supermarkets.

Curry leaves A relative of the orange blossom, these leaves have a distinctive lemon-pepper fragrance with tinges of lime and ginger. These fresh almond-shaped leaves are generally sold on the stem, and are sometimes picked and packed in plastic bags. Look for green and firm, fresh-looking leaves. Dried curry leaves, though not as fragrant, can be used, or substitute fresh coriander leaves instead.

Dried prawns These tiny, orange-coloured saltwater prawns have been dried in the sun and come in different sizes. The really small ones have their heads and tails still attached. Look for dried prawns that are pink and plump, avoiding any with a greyish appearance. The better quality ones are bright orange in colour and completely shelled. They should be soaked in warm water for several minutes to soften slightly before use. They are generally pounded in a mortar or ground in a blender to break them into smaller bits or flakes.

Fennel As a spice, the name "fennel" refers to the dried seeds of the fennel plant, although the plant itself is used as both a herb and a vegetable. The spice is elongated with an oval almond shape and is greenish to yellowish-brown in colour, looking very similar to cumin but larger and lighter in colour. It has a very distinctive, sweet taste with an aroma of aniseed and lemon and a whiff of dill. Whole and ground fennel are sold in Asian markets. Substitute aniseed or cumin.

Dried baby anchovies Also know as *ikan bilis* in Malaysia, these tiny whitebait fish are ubiquitous in South-East Asia. Dried baby anchovies are lightly salted and dried and sold either filleted, with the tiny central bone and the head removed, or whole. They are fried in a sambal with chilli, onions and garlic (see Sweet and Spicy Fish Nibbles with Peanuts, page 39) and are the main ingredient for a coconut rice dish called *nasi lemak* (page 49). Incidentally, *ikan bilis* were the main protein source for many Asians during the deprivations of the last World War.

Dried sweet Chinese sausages Also known as *xiang chang* or *lap cheong*, literally meaning "fragrant sausage," these small sweet sausages are made with pork that is flavoured with rice wine, salt, sugar and monosodium glutamate, smoked and then dried until hard. They are sold in bundles tied with red string and packaged in plastic wrappers. To use them, slice thinly and toss into stir-fries, boil or steam them, then use in fried rice or sticky rice packets. These sausages may be steamed or boiled then sliced thinly into any salad for a sweet and spicy alternative to fresh meat. Substitute beef jerky or any sweet sausage or salami.

Fish sauce This sauce is produced by layering salt with fish or prawns in earthenware vats and allowing it to ferment in the brine solution for about six months. The fermented liquid is slowly siphoned off, filtered and bottled. A top-quality fish sauce is very expensive, just like a good olive oil or vinegar. Bottles of fish sauce from various countries are available in Asian food stores and well-stocked supermarkets. Look for clear amber-coloured fish sauce, which is an indication of the best flavour and aroma. Fish sauce is used by most Asians for seasoning and marinades, while the more expensive variety is used in soups and as dipping sauces on its own or added with chilli and chopped garlic. Soy sauce with a bit of oyster sauce makes the best substitute.

Garlic chives As its name implies, garlic chives have a strong garlicky aroma and flavour. Regular garlic chives resemble coarse, flat blades of dark green grass. Garlic chives are normally sold in bunches. Look for bright green ones. They should be firm and dry, with crisp lower ends that snap if bent. They have a strong flavour when raw but become more delicate after cooking. Green onions or Western chives can be substituted but they will not give the same distinctive garlicky aroma and flavour.

Galangal One can easily mistake galangal for young ginger, for both are pinkish-cream roots that grow in knobs and put out spiky shoots. Scratch the skin and a distinctive rose and iodine-like aroma hits you, your nail does not easily penetrate the skin as it would with ginger. This rhizome feels woody and solid, and is firmer and more flavourful compared to ginger. Although galangal looks like ginger, they are not interchangeable. Scrape off the skin using a sharp knife, then chop or slice and use as instructed. As mature galangal is very tough, slice the pieces thinly first before grinding or processing them into a paste with other spices. Substitute young ginger.

Ginger The aroma of ginger is warm, peppery and subtly rose-like. Fresh

ginger is sold as young or old roots in the market. Young ginger is lighter in colour, less "spicy" and juicier than mature roots. It has pink tips, sometimes with sections of the shoots left intact. The young ginger is used sliced in delicate stir-fries and softer flavoured dishes, and as a garnish. It is also used with vinegar to make red ginger pickles, a condiment served with Japanese and Chinese dishes. The old ginger, having a more pronounced flavour that is almost hot, and a pithy, fibrous texture, is often combined with chillies, garlic and lemongrass to make a sambal. To obtain ginger juice, peel and grate the ginger using a grater, then transfer to a fine sieve and press down with the back of a spoon to extract the ginger juice. Substitute ground ginger.

Ginger flower This edible flower bud is an amazingly perfumed herb with exquisite aromas of floral ginger and lemony rose and a musk-and-strawberry sweetness. This spectacular flower is very uncommon in countries outside the tropics. The Malaysians use it quite a lot—ground up into curries and chopped up in salads—where the aroma is unmistakable in its fresh form. Look for this flower in Asian markets. Choose fresh-looking buds without too much wilting or browning at the edges. If unavailable, substitute a mixture of lemongrass and young ginger slices.

Golden syrup When cane sugar juice is reduced to produce sugar, it goes through a further refining process—golden syrup does not and still retains the flavour of the cane. Pure golden syrup is golden bown in colour and is used as a sweetener for cakes and puddings.

Hoisin sauce Recognised and used throughout Asia as the universal barbecue sauce, hoisin sauce is made from red rice brewed with soybean paste, garlic, sugar, five spice powder and some star anise. Used as a table condiment, in meat marinades and as a flavouring agent for sauces, it is famously known as the dipping sauce for Peking Duck and for roast chicken or pork barbecues, and is sometimes labelled as a dark *char siew* barbecue sauce for roast pork or duck. Hoisin sauce is sold in bottles, jars or cans in Asian markets and supermarkets. Chinese barbecue sauce or a mix of oyster sauce and tomato sauce may be substituted, although this combination never works as well as true hoisin sauce.

Jicama Also known as *bangkuang* or yam bean, these tubers have a short root and a thin papery skin that can be peeled off easily to reveal a white flesh inside that tastes like a juicy nashi pear. The peeled root is often sliced into salads as it remains crunchy without "weeping" when acidic dressings are added and does not discolour when exposed to air. It is used by the Nonyas as a spring roll filling and in the famous *rojak* salad (see Crisp *Rojak* Salad with Spicy Sweet Dressing, page 34). Peel the skin and slice the flesh into large pieces, then slice again diagonally. Depending on the recipe, substitute apple or pear.

Kaffir lime leaves These leaves are prized for their distinctive incense-like aroma and sharp citrus oils. Look for plastic packets of fresh, green and glossy kaffir lime leaves in Asian stores. Although dried or frozen leaves are available, try to use fresh leaves for their superior aroma and flavour. The fragrant leaves are added whole to soups and curries, or finely shredded and added to salads or deep-fried fish cakes, giving a wonderfully tangy taste to these dishes. When flavouring curries, use whole leaves and add them during the last minute of cooking. Dried kaffir lime leaves are a poor substitute. Young lemon, lime or even grapefruit leaves may be used as a last resort.

Lemongrass This citrus-scented, lemony herb is used all over the world wherever Thai and other South-East Asian foods are cooked. Choose firm stems that end in fat bulbs with no signs of wilting. Lemongrass is ground with garlic, galangal, onion and chilli into a paste used to make curries and soups. The entire stem, trimmed to a point, can also be used as an aromatic skewer for grilling meats and seafood. Use only the inner part of the thick bulb of the stem (the bottom one-third of the stem). Peel off and discard the

tough outer leaves to get to the portion, then bruise, slice, chop or grind as directed in the recipe. Sliced lime leaves or sliced lime or lemon rind can be substituted.

Mango You can smell a ripe mango miles away. Its aroma is a good indication of its sweetness. There is also a green mango variety that is popularly used in Asian salads with very little aroma but a great tart flavour. This mango does not sweeten but retain its tartness even when it is ripe. It has a pale green skin like a green apple, and is crisp as a choko flesh but has a wonderful sour taste with a hint of sweetness that goes well with salads. Green mangoes should be firm and without any black spots. If green mangos cannot be found for the salads in this book, perhaps you could use an unripe paw paw or crisp green apples instead. Amchoor is a dry powder made from tart green mangoes that is used to add a bite to many sour-spicy southern Indian curries.

Mint There are many varieties of mint; peppermint and spearmint are the most common. Asians prefer the type of mint which has dark-green, crinkly round leaves, sometimes called

Moroccan mint. Asians also use spearmint—the Vietnamese add them to bowls of *pho* noodles. Look for fresh leaves on green stems, with strong aromas of mint. Use 1 tablespoon dried mint leaves in place of 10 g ($^1/_4$ cup) fresh leaves.

Mirin A strong, sweet rice wine with a smoky woody flavour of mushrooms that lifts any dish, mirin is used extensively in Japan and now the world over. It is brewed from sweet sticky (glutinous) short-grained rice and matured for at least five years before it is bottled and sold commercially. The main characteristic of mirin is a sweet aroma which comes from the addition of corn syrup and alcohol. Mirin is normally found in Japanese stores, but any good Asian store will stock it. Sherry or white wine or sake with a little sugar added, or Shaoxing wine with added sugar makes a good substitute.

Oyster sauce and oyster mushroom sauce Brewed from the natural salting of fish or oysters in seaside areas, oyster sauce is one of the earliest sauces used in Chinese cooking. The fishy taste of the sauce dissipates when it is cooked, leaving only an aroma and flavour so elegant and tasty that it is used by cooks now throughout the whole of Asia. Today this sauce is made from dried oysters mixed with salt and sugar that caramelises into a flavoursome end product. Vegetarians should look for a version sold as "mushroom oyster sauce", this is flavoured with gluten and mushrooms rather than oyster extract. Check the label to see what it contains—many oyster sauces contain added MSG. Fish sauce mixed with *kecap manis* or sweet soy sauce is a good substitute.

Essential Malaysian Ingredients

Palm sugar is distilled from the sap of various palm fruits. It is usually sold as a solid block or cylinder. It varies in colour from gold to light brown and has a faint caramel taste. Palm sugar should be shaved, grated or melted in a microwave oven before measuring it. Substitute dark brown sugar or maple syrup.

Pandanus leaves The pandanus leaves are narrow, spear-like and pliant, with a firm central vein. Their distinctive and subtle grassy aroma is only released when the leaves are bruised, twisted or ground into a paste. Pandanus leaves are usually sold in a bundle in Asian markets. But they are either sold frozen or in powdered form in other parts of the world. In Malaysia, pandanus leaves are mainly used for their fragrance in desserts and meat and rice dishes, while the green juice is also used to provide a bright green colour to foods. To prepare pandanus juice, slice several leaves and grind them in a mortar or food processor until fine, then strain, squeezing out the juice. Substitute lemongrass if pandanus leaves are unavailable.

Pepper and Sichuan pepper Black pepper is the fruit of the pepper vine. The berries are harvested whilst still unripe and dried on mats in the sun until they become the dark peppercorns we know. White pepper is made by husking ripe berries picked when they are red or orange, then soaking them in running water, washing again and drying them. Black pepper is the whole berry with the husk left on, which has a stronger taste. The shiny aromatic black seeds with magenta husks known as Sichuan pepper are not true peppercorns but the berries of a bush found in the Sichuan region of China. They have a subtle warming taste and a lemon-lime aroma that lingers on the tongue and produces a slight numbing effect similar to that of cloves when chewed. When dry-roasted and crushed, they add a warm spicy flavour to roast chicken and to duck and pork dishes. Sichuan pepper is available in clear pepper shakers in Japanese supermarkets. The obvious substitute for pepper is to use a touch of chilli, either in dried powdered form, or chilli flakes.

Pineapple There are many varieties of pineapple, ranging from the large green Hawaiian variety to the dimunitive yellow-orange Asian variety. Ripe pineapple is a favourite table fruit and its juice can be strained and added to cocktails. It is the semi-ripe pineapple that is often used in cooking. Use canned pineapple if fresh pineapple is not available.

Dried black Chinese mushrooms

Woodear fungus

Mushrooms are grown commercially throughout Asia and are highly sought after. Dried black Chinese mushrooms are similar to shiitake mushrooms but must be soaked in water before use. Woodear fungus, also known as cloud ear fungus, is a crinkly greyish-brown dried mushroom that swells to many times its original size after being soaked in warm water for a few minutes. They have little flavour but are prized for their texture.

Plum sauce This sauce adds an aromatic fruitiness to marinades and meat and fish dishes and is commonly used as a dipping sauce. Plum sauce is a sweet and tart Chinese sauce made from small, sour Chinese plums preserved with sugar and molasses until it becomes light and aromatic. Plum and chilli sauce in equal amounts forms a good dipping sauce for finger foods. Fried onions added to a bottle of plum jam is a great substitute for plum sauce. If it is too sweet add a tablespoon of lime juice.

Prawn paste, dried and wet Fresh prawns, fish and krill are used to make this basic paste which is added to almost every Malaysian dish. Dry-roasted dried prawn paste is aromatic, yeasty and smoky, reminiscent of barbecued fish and prawns. It is known as *belachan* in Malaysia. Wet prawn paste, *petis* or *hae koh*, is a liquid prawn paste sold in jars and has a much stronger fish taste than the dried version. Dried prawn paste is usually sold as a dark brown compressed block wrapped with paper or plastic and should always be dry-roasted before using. You can dry-roast a solid chunk by holding it with a pair of tongs or wrapping it in foil and roasting it over a flame to dissipate the fishy aromas. Or you can dry-roast it in a microwave oven for 1 minute on high. Substitute fish sauce with some oyster sauce added if necessary.

Preserved Chinese cabbage Also known as *tang chye*, this is made from Chinese or Napa cabbage which is shredded

and then salted and dried. It turns golden brown once preserved. It is slightly moist, with a salty flavour and crunchy texture. It is often sprinkled on rice porridge and is sometimes used to garnish noodle dishes.

Rice stick noodles Also known as *horfun*, river noodles or *kway teow*, these noodles are produced fresh in most Chinatowns and are also available as dried noodles in plastic bags in all Asian food stores. There are two sizes, one slightly thicker and wider than the other. The larger flat noodle is used in stir fries (see Bean Sauce Noodles with Prawns and Sausage, page 54), in soups or in steamed noodle recipes, while the narrower noodle is used in Thai noodle dishes, for instance the famous Pad Thai.

Rice wine and Chinese rice wine These wines are usually made from rice, but sometimes from other grains such as sorghum or millet. The most common Chinese rice wine is the Chinese Shaoxing, which is fermented from sticky glutinous rice, yeast and water. A finely aged golden Shaoxing wine can be expensive, and can release the fruity flavours of a sweet Muscat wine. The best known Shaoxing wine

is Hua Tiao Chiew. Shaoxing is available in most Asian stores and investing in a better quality Shaoxing wine will enhance your cooking. A good sherry or mirin can be substituted.

Saffron One of the most expensive spice in the world, saffron is the stigma of a crocus flower that grows in the Middle East and Northern India. Look for even-coloured threads with vivid dark-gold and red hues, some are curly and some with a thicker head. Saffron are sold whole in tiny plastic boxes. It imparts a warm sunshine yellow colour and subtle jasmine-like perfume to any dish it is cooked in. Saffron is best added to rice after soaking a few threads in warmed milk to release its colour.

Sesame oil Extracted from sesame seeds, sesame oil comes in a range of colours—from clear to orange to red or dark amber—depending on the method used for extraction. The nutty and smoky taste of sesame oil adds depth to many vegetarian and herbal dishes. Look for bottles of sesame oil in most supermarkets. Ground dry-roasted sesame seeds added to regular cooking oil may be used as a substitute.

| Regular or light soy sauce | Dark soy sauce | Sweet soy sauce (*kecap manis*) |

Soy sauces Regular or light soy sauce is clear and golden brown in colour and slightly salty in flavour, with a yeasty aroma. Dark soy sauce is darker and slightly thicker, with a sweet and wheaty flavour. Light soy sauce is used for marinades, as dips, and for flavouring white meat and seafood. Indonesian thick sweet soy sauce (*kecap manis)* is a dark, sweet, reddish black thick soy sauce used specifically for Indonesian and Malaysian cooking. It is sweeter than ordinary soy sauce and used for rice stick noodle dishes (especially *char kway teow*), to flavour and colour meat dishes or for cooking red meat.

Star anise This spice is actually the seed pod of a small oriental tree. It is star-shaped, usually with eight radiating pointed sections. These hard sections reveal small, shiny black seeds when they are split open. It is always sold as whole pods in its dried form. Do not confuse this spice with aniseed, which is different. Substitute equal parts of cloves and cinnamon.

Starfruit This fruit has a waxy green skin which turns yellow as it ripens.

Look for unblemished firm and shiny, even-coloured fruits with green edges along the ridges. Avoid fruits with brown, shriveled ribs. Rinse it well and shave off the tops and edges of the ridges, then use as instructed in the recipe. Firm kiwi fruit may be substituted.

Tamarind The tamarind fruit grows in pods. When unripe, the pods are green but as they mature, they became brittle and brown and contain a brown-golden flesh with large seeds and fibres. The pulp is often puréed and sold in a block, in jars or bottles. This is used as a souring agent for soups, curries, stews, salads, dressings and sauces. Always taste the tamarind before deciding how much to use. To make tamarind juice, break off a chunk of the pulp from the dried tamarind block and mix it with some warm water. Mash the mixture with your

fingers to break up the pulp until it is fully dissolved to form a thick, reddish brown liquid or paste. Strain the mixture through a fine sieve to obtain the juice. Discard the fibrous husks and seeds. Substitute 2 dates puréed with 2 tablespoon fresh lime juice for 1 tablespoon of tamarind juice.

Tempeh is made by culturing boiled soybeans in the same way that cheese is made from cultured milk solids. It is a vital and inexpensive meat substitute for Indonesians and Malaysians who live on a rice and vegetable diet with little meat. Tempeh has 40% more protein and far more vitamins and minerals than meat. Substitute firm tofu or pressed tofu if you cannot find it.

Thai basil Asian basils come in three different varieties—Thai basil, lemon scented basil and holy basil. The most common of the three has an intense aroma and is generally known as Thai basil (*daun kemangi* in Malaysia and Indonesia). Look for brightly-coloured, fresh basil with leaves that stand firm, without any hint of wilting. Wash and dry the leaves well. Tender leaves can be used but separate the leaves from the harder stems. European basil is a good substitute though it may not have as much bite and aroma as the Asian basil.

Turmeric The rhizome of a ginger-like plant, this root resembles ginger but is much smaller and thinner, and the caterpillar-shaped tubers are covered with a thin brownish skin that lets the bright orange-yellow flesh inside show through. Although turmeric is widely used in India and outside Asia in its dried ground form, the fresh root is preferred in Malaysia for its fragrance, flavour and bright yellow colour. Both fresh roots and ground turmeric are sold in Asian markets. Turmeric is always used in very small amounts, to colour and flavour dishes and to mask unwanted aromas. Take care not to get the juice on your clothing as it will stain permanently. When fresh turmeric root is not available, use ground turmeric.

Vietnamese mint This leaf is not really a mint but a closer relative to basil than to coriander or mint. The dark-green, almond-shaped leaves are long and tapering with a bright green colour and a distinctive dark red or green "arrow" shape in the centre. Look for dark green leaves in firm bunches with a fresh aroma. They should look plump and fresh, without any signs of bruising. Strip the leaves and tender stalks from the central stem before using. Equal parts of mint and coriander leaves or Asian penny-wort may be used as a substitute.

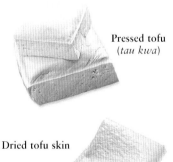

Pressed tofu (*tau kwa*)

Dried tofu skin

Tofu or **beancurd** comes in many different forms. **Pressed tofu** (often confusingly labelled as firm tofu) is a type of firm tofu with much of the water pressed out of it and is therefore much firmer in texture and excellent for stir-fries. Refrigerate fresh tofu enclosed in a plastic container submerged in water. **Dried tofu skin** is the dried skin that forms on top of boiling soybean milk. It is dried and sold in sheets as a spring roll wrapper.

Turmeric leaves Also known as *daun kunyit*, these leaves are highly aromatic and impart a delicious flavour to many dishes. Like turmeric root, the leaves also have many health benefits in aiding digestion, fighting bacteria and cleansing the system. The leaves are used as herb, particularly in Sumatra. There is no substitute.

Wolfberries Also known by their Japanese name, *goji* or "red berries," these dried berries have a pleasant sweet-sour flavour and are often added to soups, especially chicken soup. Available at most Chinese herbalists. If unavailable, use dried cranberries.

Chilli Sambal

Sambal Oelek Chilli Paste

SAMBALS, CHUTNEYS, SPICE PASTES AND ACHARS

Chilli sambal

This is a favourite recipe that can be made up and heated for use later and will make a great Christmas gift when bottled.

2 tablespoons oil
4 cloves garlic, crushed
1 medium onion, chopped
1$^1/_2$ tablespoons Sambal Oelek Chilli Paste (recipe on this page) or other sweet chilli paste
60 g ($^1/_2$ cup) dried prawns, rinsed and dry-roasted
1 tablespoon tamarind pulp, mashed in $^1/_4$ cup (60 ml) water and strained to obtain the juice
50 g ($^1/_4$ cup) dark brown sugar or shaved palm sugar
1 tablespoon fish sauce
Salt, to taste

Heat the oil in a skillet and sauté the garlic, onion and Sambal Oelek over medium heat until fragrant, 1–2 minutes. Add all the other ingredients, except the salt, and sauté until the volume reduces to half, 3–5 minutes. Season with salt to taste and remove from the heat. Cool and store refrigerated in a sealed jar.

MAKES: *1 cup*   PREPARATION: *20 mins*
COOKING: *10 mins*

Sambal oelek chilli paste

The action of grinding a chilli paste is "oelek" or "ulek" in Malay. Commercial brands like the Indonesian ABC brand are good, but this sauce is so simple to make that you should try it. If you have a blender it becomes a simple process, but remember to bring it to the boiling point and cool before storing.

1 onion, peeled and sliced
5 cloves garlic, peeled
2.5 cm (1 in) fresh ginger, peeled and thinly sliced
12 red finger-length chillies, halved and deseeded
2 tablespoons oil
1 teaspoon shaved palm sugar or dark brown sugar
$^3/_8$ cup (100 ml) vinegar
$^1/_4$ teaspoon salt, to taste

Grind the onion, garlic, ginger and chillies in a food processor or mortar to a smooth paste. Heat the oil in a skillet and sauté the ground paste over medium heat until fragrant, 3–5 minutes, seasoning with the sugar, vinegar and salt.

Remove from the heat and cool, then store refrigerated in a sealed jar for up to 2 months.

MAKES: *1 cup*   PREPARATION TIME: *10 mins*
COOKING TIME: *5 mins*

Cucumber mint raita

This is an Indian side dish that is used to "smother" the flames of a spicy curry or other main dish. Use it also as a salad dressing. I often throw in a peeled banana to make an unusual dessert!

1 baby cucumber, peeled, cored and diced
1 teaspoon salt
1 semi-ripe tomato, diced
1 onion, finely chopped
$3/4$ cup (180 ml) plain yoghurt
1 green finger-length chilli, deseeded and finely chopped
20 g ($1/2$ cup) mint leaves, chopped

Sprinkle the cucumber with the salt and mix well. Allow to stand for 30 minutes, then drain and squeeze the liquid from the cucumber. Add all the other ingredients and mix well.

Note: For a creamier version, substitute the same amount of coconut cream for the yoghurt.

MAKES: *1$1/2$ cups*   **PREPARATION TIME:** *20 mins*

Mint pachidi chutney

Minty and garlicky and deliciously reminiscent of coconut macaroons. Serve it as a condiment with roast meat, or as a relish with rice or roti.

1 tablespoon oil
1 onion, chopped
2 cloves garlic, sliced
12 mm ($1/2$ in) fresh ginger, cut into thin shreds
4 green finger-length chillies, deseeded and sliced
2 tablespoons dried unsweetened grated (desiccated) coconut, dry-roasted until golden brown
80 g (2 cups) fresh mint leaves, washed and dried
Freshly squeezed juice of 2 limes
Salt, to taste

Heat the oil in a wok and stir-fry the onion, garlic and ginger over medium heat until golden and tender. Add the chilli and coconut and stir-fry for 1 minute, then remove from the heat. Process the coconut mixture with the mint leaves in a food processor until smooth. Transfer to a bowl and add the lime juice and salt to taste. Cover and chill until ready to serve. It keeps refrigerated for 3–4 days.

MAKES: *1$1/2$ cups*   **PREPARATION TIME:** *20 mins*
COOKING TIME: *5 mins*

Cucumber Mint Raita

Mint Pachidi Chutney

Sweet tamarind date chutney

This recipe was given to me by a friend who comes from a Cape Malay family from Cape Town, South Africa. They cook very interesting foods similar to our Malaysian kormas and pilaffs.

100 g ($^1/_3$ cup) chopped pitted dates, or chopped pitted dates with whole raisins
2 teaspoons fennel seeds, dry-roasted and ground to a powder in a mortar or spice grinder
1 tablespoon ground red pepper, or to taste
150 g ($^1/_2$ cup) tamarind pulp mashed in 1 cup (250 ml) water and strained to obtain the juice
65 g ($^1/_3$ cup) dark brown sugar or jaggery
Salt, to taste
1 tablespoon oil
$^1/_2$ teaspoon mustard seeds
35 g ($^1/_4$ cup) chopped roasted macadamia nuts

Process the dates, fennel seeds, ground red pepper, tamarind juice, sugar and salt to a purée in a food processor. Heat the oil in a wok and stir-fry the mustard seeds over high heat until they pop, 1–2 minutes. Add the purée and bring to a boil, stirring constantly until the chutney becomes thick, 2–3 minutes. Reduce the heat to low and simmer uncovered for about 2 more minutes. When the chutney has a dropping consistency, stir well and remove from the heat. Stir in the macadamia nuts and serve immediately. Store the unused chutney in a sealed jar in the refrigerator, after cooling.

MAKES: $^3/_4$ cup   **PREPARATION TIME:** *30 mins*
COOKING TIME: *10 mins*

Aromatic Nonya Spice Paste

Sweet Tamarind Date Chutney

Aromatic nonya spice paste

This curry paste is the classic Nonya standby. Use it as base for many Nonya curries and laksa dishes. Double the quantity as a time-saving exercise and use it as a stir-fry starter for vegetables and soups instead of starting with chopped garlic and onions.

1 medium onion, chopped
2 stalks lemongrass, thick bottom part only, outer layers discarded, inner part sliced
10 red finger-length chillies, halved and deseeded
1 tablespoon dried prawns
2 candlenuts or macadamia nuts
2 tablespoons oil
1 tablespoon fresh lime juice
2 teaspoons shaved palm sugar or dark brown sugar
2 tablespoons water
$^1/_2$ teaspoon salt or fish sauce, to taste

Grind the onion, lemongrass, chilli, dried prawns and candlenuts or macadamia in a food processor or mortar until smooth.

Heat the oil in a wok and stir-fry the paste over medium heat until fragrant, 1–2 minutes. Add the lime juice, sugar and water, mix well and bring to a boil, then simmer uncovered, stirring, for 2–3 minutes until the mixture thickens. Season with salt to taste and remove from the heat. Cool and store refrigerated in a sealed jar.

MAKES: *1 cup*   **PREPARATION TIME:** *45 mins*
COOKING TIME: *5 mins*

Lemongrass paste

Lemongrass is an aromatic herb used for centuries in South-East Asia. It may be sliced very finely as garnish, but in this case, this interesting paste is used for many of my curries or laksa dishes, as it has the freshness of ginger and galangal, and the aroma of kaffir lime.

4 stalks lemongrass, thick bottom part only, outer layers discarded, inner parts sliced
2.5 cm (1 in) fresh galangal root, peeled and sliced
10 cloves garlic, peeled
12 mm ($^1/_2$ in) fresh ginger, peeled and sliced
12 red finger-length chillies, halved and deseeded
1 tablespoon dried prawns, dry-roasted
1 tablespoon oil
2 teaspoons shaved palm sugar or dark brown sugar
4 tablespoons water
1 kaffir lime leaf, cut into thin strips
$^1/_2$ teaspoon salt, or to taste

Grind the lemongrass, galangal, garlic, ginger and chillies in a food processor or mortar until fine. Add the dried prawns and grind to a smooth paste.

Heat the oil in a skillet and sauté the paste over medium heat until fragrant, 2–3 minutes. Stir in all the other ingredients, except the salt, and simmer uncovered for 3–5 minutes, stirring constantly until the mixture thickens. Season with salt to taste and remove from the heat, cool and store refrigerated in a sealed jar.

MAKES: *1 cup*   PREPARATION TIME: *30 mins*
COOKING TIME: *10 mins*

Lemongrass Paste

Fish curry powder

The difference between a fish and a meat curry powder is a couple of spices that add sourness and aroma to the fish curries. You may choose a commercial blend or make your own using a little less or more fenugreek seeds, mustard and some lime juice to hold the powder together.

3 tablespoons coriander seeds
1 teaspoon cumin seeds
4 teaspoons fennel seeds
4 dried red finger-length chillies, stems discarded, broken into pieces
2 teaspoons fenugreek seeds
1 teaspoon mustard seeds

In a skillet, dry-roast each of the whole spices separately over gentle heat until fragrant, 2–3 minutes each. Let them cool and then grind all the spices to a fine powder in a mortar or spice grinder. Store in a sealed jar refrigerated or frozen.

MAKES: $^1/_2$ *cup*   PREPARATION TIME: *10 mins*
COOKING TIME: *10 mins*

Meat curry powder

Normally curry powders are freshly made by cooks who have the time to measure out each spice and dry roast it before grinding them all into a paste or powder. It may be convenient to use a commercial blend like "Baba" curry powders, but it is more satisfying to make your own and vary the ingredients as needed.

3 tablespoons coriander seeds
4 teaspoons cumin seeds
$^1/_2$ tablespoon fennel seeds
4 dried red finger-length chillies, stems discarded, broken into pieces
1 teaspoon fenugreek seeds
$^1/_2$ teaspoon mustard seeds
1 teaspoon ground cinnamon
1 teaspoon ground nutmeg
1 teaspoon ground cloves

In a skillet, dry-roast each of the whole spices separately over gentle heat until fragrant, 2–3 minutes each. Let them cool and then grind all the spices to a fine powder in a mortar or spice grinder. Store in a sealed jar refrigerated or frozen.

MAKES: $^1/_2$ *cup*   PREPARATION TIME: *10 mins*
COOKING TIME: *10 mins*

Crispy fried garlic

2 tablespoons oil
3–4 cloves garlic, peeled and minced

Heat the oil in a skillet and sauté the garlic over medium heat until golden and crispy, about 1 minute. Remove from the oil and drain on paper towels.

To make sliced Crispy Fried Garlic, peel and thinly sliced, instead of mincing, the garlic cloves.

MAKES: *3 tablespoons*   **PREPARATION TIME:** *5 mins*
COOKING TIME: *5 mins*

Green onion curls

2–3 green onions
Bowl of iced water

To make Green Onion Curls, trim off the bulb of each green onion at the point where the stem begins to turn green. Slice the leaves into 10-cm (4-in) lengths. Using a sharp knife, slice each length into very thin strips lengthwise. Soak the strips in a bowl of iced water and refrigerate until they curl up.

Vegetable stock

A vegetable stock may be made from any vegetables that you can have on hand, but the root vegetables give more flavour, especially onions and carrots, and a stick of celery. I use red dhal as a thickener for these stocks, as they also add flavour, but you may use potatoes as a thickener instead.

4 cups (1 litre) water
2 cloves garlic, bruised
1 onion, cut into wedges
2 carrots, peeled and chopped
100 g (^{1}/$_2$ cup) red (mysore) dhal
1 cup (250 ml) water

Bring all the ingredients to a boil in a stockpot. Reduce the heat to low and simmer partially covered for 30 minutes, skimming off the residue that floats to the surface. Remove from the heat, strain through a fine sieve and discard the solids. Allow the clear stock to cool completely before refrigerating or freezing.

MAKES: *2^1/$_2$ cups (625 ml)*   **PREPARATION TIME:** *5 mins*
COOKING TIME: *30 mins*

Chicken stock

Make friends with your butcher to obtain the boned carcass of chickens or the knuckle joints and make them into a stock, using some vegetables and some ginger to add flavour. Meat stocks including chicken should be cooked for at least 1 hour, to obtain the best flavour. Remove the residue that floats to the top as it cooks.

8 cups (2 litres) water
1 kg (2 lbs) chicken bones or ^{1}/$_2$ fresh chicken
1 small onion or 3 green onions (scallions), chopped
1 celery, sliced
6 black peppercorns, freshly cracked
5 cloves garlic, chopped
2.5 cm (1 in) fresh ginger, peeled and bruised
2 stalks lemongrass, thick part only, outer layers discarded, inner part bruised

Bring all the ingredients to a rolling boil for about 5 minutes in a stockpot. Reduce the heat to low and simmer uncovered for 30 minutes, skimming off the residue and fat that float to the surface. Increase the heat and return to a boil for 10 minutes then remove from the heat. Strain through a fine sieve and discard the solids. Allow the clear stock to cool completely before refrigerating or freezing.

MAKES: *6 cups (1.5 litres)*   **PREPARATION TIME:** *20 mins*
COOKING TIME: *45 mins*

Fish stock

Simple to make if you have leftover fish bones or prawn shells, and certainly more authentic than using commercially prepared fish stocks which may contain MSG. I use *amchoor* or mango powder for a change instead of lime juice. This stock only needs ^{1}/$_2$ hour of cooking.

4 cups (1 litre) water
300 g (10 oz) fish bones, or fish head, cleaned well
2 teaspoons dried mango powder (*amchoor*), or
   300 g (10 oz) prawn shells
1 green onion (scallion)

Bring all the ingredients to a boil in a stockpot. Reduce the heat to low and simmer partially covered for 30 minutes, skimming off the residue that floats to the surface. Remove from the heat, strain through a fine sieve and discard the solids. Allow the clear stock to cool completely before refrigerating or freezing.

MAKES: *2^1/$_2$ cups (625 ml)*   **PREPARATION TIME:** *5 mins*
COOKING TIME: *25 mins*

Nonya pickled vegetables with dried prawns

The Nonya (Straits Chinese) version of *achar* (a word of Indian origin that means "pickles") is made with crunchy vegetables marinated in a punchy mixture of vinegar and spices that produce delightful sweet and sour aromas and textures. Served in small bowls as a side dish, this *achar* goes well with meat dishes.

400 g (14 oz) green beans, sliced into short lengths
3 baby gherkins or pickling cucumbers, cut into half length-wise, cored and sliced into small batons
2 carrots, peeled and sliced into small batons
400 g (3 cups) tiny cauliflower florets
2 cups (500 ml) white vinegar
Salt, to taste
3 tablespoons oil
1 teaspoon ground turmeric
1 small onion, diced
5 cloves garlic, peeled
2.5 cm (1 in) fresh ginger, peeled and thinly sliced
2 stalks lemongrass, thick bottom part only, outer layers discarded, inner parts sliced
1 teaspoon dried prawn paste (*belachan*)
1 teaspoon sugar
Salt, to taste
2 tablespoons dry-roasted sesame seeds

STUFFED CHILLIES
3 red finger-length chillies
2 tablespoons dried prawns, coarsely ground in a mortar or blender
1 tablespoon Sambal Oelek Chilli Paste (page 26) or other sweet chilli paste
1 tablespoon shaved palm sugar or dark brown sugar

Sprinkle each type of vegetable with ½ a teaspoon of salt separately and mix well. Allow them to stand for 1 hour, then drain and squeeze out all the liquid from the vegetables. Set aside.

To prepare the Stuffed Chillies, make a slit length-wise on one side of each chilli with a paring knife, but do not cut through. Using a teaspoon, scoop out and discard the pith and seeds from the inside of each chilli to form a pocket for stuffing.

Combine the dried prawns, Sambal Oelek Chilli Paste and sugar in a dish and mix well, then microwave for about 2 minutes until crisp, stopping to stir the mixture every 30 seconds. Stuff 1 teaspoon of the roasted dried prawns mixture into each chilli pepper and set aside.

Bring the vinegar and a little salt to a boil over medium heat in a saucepan and blanch each of the vegetables separately for 30 seconds to 1 minute. Remove from the heat, drain each vegetable and place in a glass bowl together with the Stuffed Chillies. Reserve the vinegar mixture used for blanching the vegetables.

Heat the oil in a wok and stir-fry the ground turmeric over medium heat for 30 seconds. Add the onion, garlic and ginger, and stir-fry until golden brown, 1–2 minutes. Stir in the lemongrass and prawn paste and toss until fragrant. Add ¼ cup (60 ml) of the reserved vinegar mixture and season with the sugar and salt to taste. Bring the vinegar mixture to a boil. The mixture should be reddish yellow and not caramelised. Stir in all the vegetables and Stuffed Chillies and turn off the heat, then toss thoroughly to mix well. Transfer the *achar* to several clean glass jars and sprinkle about 1 teaspoon of the sesame seeds on top of each jar. Seal and store refrigerated for up to 1 year.

MAKES: *3 cups*   **PREPARATION TIME:** *1 hour + 1 hour for the vegetables to stand*   **COOKING TIME:** *10 mins*

Cashew nut satay sauce

Most satay sauces use peanuts. As many people have peanut allergies, I have created an alternative version using dry-roasted cashew nuts instead.

125 g (1 cup) raw cashew nuts or peanuts
3 tablespoons oil
3 cloves garlic, minced
1 onion, finely chopped
1 stalk lemongrass, thick part only, outer layers discarded, inner part sliced
2 tablespoons Meat Curry Powder (page 29)
1 tablespoon Sambal Oelek Chilli Paste (page 26)
1 tablespoon tamarind pulp, mashed with ½ cup (125 ml) water, strained to obtain the juice
2 tablespoons milk powder
2 cups (500 ml) hot water
1½ tablespoons sugar
2 tablespoons plum sauce
1 teaspoon salt, or to taste

Dry-roast the cashew nuts or peanuts in a skillet over low heat, stirring continuously for 2–3 minutes until they are a golden colour and cooked. Then coarsely grind them in a mortar or blender and set aside. Heat the oil in a wok and stir-fry the garlic, onion and lemongrass over medium heat until fragrant, 1–2 minutes. Add the curry powder, Sambal Oelek and tamarind juice and bring to a boil, then simmer uncovered for about 2 minutes. Stir in the cashew nuts or peanuts, milk powder and hot water and cook over medium-low heat until the sauce thickens, 3–5 minutes. Reduce the heat to low, season with the sugar, plum sauce and salt and remove from the heat.

MAKES: *2 cups (500 ml)*   **PREPARATION TIME:** *30 mins*
COOKING TIME: *10 mins*

SAMBALS, CHUTNEYS, SPICE PASTES AND ACHARS

salads and
snacks

2 cakes (each 150 g/5 oz) pressed firm
    tofu, cubed and deep-fried
2 Chinese fried bread sticks (*yu tiao*, see
    note), sliced or 60 g (1 cup) croutons
1 cucumber, halved lengthwise and thinly
    sliced
1 small jicama, peeled and sliced into thin
    wedges
1 ripe fresh pineapple, peeled, cored and
    sliced into chunks
1 unripe green mango, peeled, pitted and
    sliced
2 medium starfruits, sliced
1 tablespoon dry-roasted sesame seeds
2 tablespoons crushed dry-roasted peanuts
    or cashew nuts
Grated lime rind, to garnish (optional)

SPICY SWEET ROJAK DRESSING
2 tablespoons boiling water
$1^1/_2$ tablespoons black sweet prawn paste
    (*hae koh*)
2–3 tablespoons sugar
2 teaspoons Sambal Oelek Chilli Paste
    (page 26) or other sweet chilli paste
1 tablespoon oyster sauce
Fresh juice of 1 lime
$^1/_4$ teaspoon salt, or to taste

Crisp *rojak* salad with spicy sweet dressing

A ubiquitous classic, this tossed crisp salad known as *rojak* is a tumbled blend of bold aromas—the glistening black molasses-like prawn dressing and roasted peanuts overpower everything else with their strong aromas. But take a bite and you will release the crisp scented flavours of green mango, ripe sweet pineapple and fresh jicama chunks that give texture to this salad, and a special sweet, tart and pungent taste that no other Asian salad provides. So prepare to be seduced by the most exciting salad imaginable as you crunch each mouthful, evoking memories of good food and colourful markets in Malaysia. This cold dish is eaten as a snack or appetiser in Malaysia and Singapore, and needs no accompaniments.

Prepare the Sambal Oelek Chilli Paste by following the recipe on page 26.

Prepare the Spicy Sweet Rojak Dressing first by adding boiling water to the black sweet prawn paste in a bowl and mixing well. Add the sugar and stir until the sugar is dissolved, then stir in all the other ingredients, adjusting the taste.

Place all the salad ingredients in a large bowl, drizzle the Spicy Sweet Rojak Dressing over them and toss thoroughly until the salad is well coated with the dressing. Transfer to individual serving plates, sprinkle with the sesame seeds, ground peanuts or cashews, and serve immediately garnished with grated lime rind.

Note: Chinese fried bread sticks (*yu tiao*) are dough strips that are deep-fried into puffy, crisp sticks. The Chinese usually have them with coffee or congee for breakfast. They can be found fresh in Chinese food stores and well-stocked Malaysian supermarkets. If unavailable, substitute crisp bread croutons.

SERVES: *6*　　PREPARATION TIME: *30 mins*

500 g (1 lb) boneless chicken thigh fillets,
sliced into 20 long, narrow strips
20 bamboo skewers, soaked in water for
1 hour to prevent them from burning
$^1/_4$ cup (60 ml) coconut cream
2 tablespoons oil
2 teaspoons shaved palm sugar or dark
brown sugar
Cucumber slices, to serve
Onion wedges, to serve
1 portion Cashew Nut Satay Sauce (page 31),
to dip

MARINADE
1 tablespoon Amah's Curry Powder (page 62)
2 tablespoons Lemongrass Paste (page 29)
1 teaspoon ground turmeric
1 teaspoon cumin seeds, dry-roasted and
ground
3 tablespoons shaved palm sugar or dark
brown sugar, mixed with $^1/_2$ cup (125 ml)
hot water

Chicken satay with fragrant spices

Chicken Satay is everyone's favourite—delicate barbecued morsels with an enticing fragrance of caramelised palm sugar, coconut cream and grilling chicken. A food fit for the Gods!.

Prepare the Lemongrass Paste and Amah's Curry Powder by following the recipes on pages 29 and 62. Combine these with the other Marinade ingredients in a shallow dish and mix well. Thread each chicken strip on a soaked bamboo skewer, in a zig-zag pattern. Place all the skewers in the dish with the Marinade, coating the chicken pieces well with the Marinade. Cover and refrigerate for at least 2 hours.

Prepare the Cashew Nut Satay Sauce by following the recipe on page 31.

Make a basting sauce by combining the coconut cream, oil and palm sugar in a small bowl and mixing well. Set aside.

Grill the skewers on a preheated pan grill, under a broiler or over a charcoal fire for 2–3 minutes on each side until cooked, constantly basting with the basting sauce. When they are done, arrange the satays on a platter on a bed of sliced cucumber and onion wedges, and serve hot with bowls of Cashew Nut Satay Sauce on the side.

MAKES: *20 satays*   **PREPARATION TIME:** *45 mins + marination time*   **COOKING TIME :** *20 mins*

20 chicken wings, mid-portion only
125 g (1 cup) rice flour or crushed corn flakes
1 pandanus leaf, torn lengthwise into long
   strips (optional)

PLUM SAUCE MARINADE
2 tablespoons bottled sweet chilli sauce
4 tablespoons plum sauce
1 tablespoon dark soy sauce
1 tablespoon honey
2 tablespoons fresh lime juice
1 teaspoon salt
$1/2$ teaspoon ground white pepper

TANGY LIME GINGER DIP
Fresh juice of 2 limes
2 teaspoons sugar
1 teaspoon Sambal Oelek Chilli Paste
   (page 26) or other sweet chilli paste
2 teaspoons ginger juice (pressed from
   grated fresh ginger)

Plum sauce chicken wings baked in a flash

This is an interactive recipe where you can have fun. If some of the sauces are unavailable, clean out your refrigerator and create your own sensual combination by adding a cocktail of sauces for fragrance and taste. The wings make a great finger food when served with a delicate dipping sauce. For a really fragrant alternative, tie strips of pandanus leaf around the chicken wings; the leaf will brown but the flavour remains.

Prepare the Sambal Oelek Chilli Paste by following the recipe on page 26.

Combine the Plum Sauce Marinade ingredients in a large bowl and mix well. Add the chicken wings and mix until well coated. Allow to marinate for at least 2 hours.

Preheat the oven to 170°C (340°F).

Roll the marinated wings in the rice flour or corn flakes to coat on all sides, shaking off the excess flour or flakes. Tie a pandanus leaf strip around each coated wing (if using). Place the chicken wings on a large greased baking pan and bake in the oven for 15 minutes, then turn over and bake for another 10 minutes until done. If preferred, grill the chicken wings on a preheated pan grill or under a broiler for 5–10 minutes on each side, checking often to make sure the chicken does not burn.

Combine the Tangy Lime Ginger Dip ingredients in a serving bowl and mix well. Arrange the baked chicken wings on a serving platter and serve with the dip on the side.

MAKES: *20*   **PREPARATION TIME:** *20 mins*   **COOKING TIME:** *25 mins*

125 g (2 cups) dried baby anchovies (*Ikan bilis*) or whitebaits, heads and intestines removed, rinsed, then drained well
Oil, for frying

AROMATIC SAMBAL
3 tablespoons oil
4 tablespoons Chilli Sambal (page 26)
4 tablespoons Aromatic Nonya Spice Paste (page 28)
6 candlenuts or macadamia nuts, crushed or ground
4 teaspoons dried prawns, dry-roasted and ground in a blender or mortar
1 tablespoon tamarind pulp, mashed with $^1/_2$ cup (125 ml) water and strained to obtain the juice
2 teaspoons tomato ketchup
2 teaspoons fresh lime juice
2 teaspoons sugar, or to taste
$^1/_2$ teaspoon salt, or to taste
$^1/_2$ cup (125 ml) coconut cream

Crunchy ikan bilis with aromatic sambal

Baby anchovies or ikan bilis fished along the coasts of South-East Asia are dazzling silver flakes when dried on mats in the sun. They are used not only in sambals but also in crunchy nibbles. Here the assertive flavours of chilli, lemongrass and tamarind in the dip create a seductive snack.

Prepare the Chilli Sambal and Aromatic Nonya Spice Paste by following the recipes on pages 26 and 28.

Remove and discard the heads and intestines from the anchovies, then rinse well and pat dry with paper towels. Heat the oil in a wok until hot and fry the anchovies or whitebaits over medium heat until golden brown and crispy, 2–3 minutes. Remove from the heat and drain on paper towels. Keep warm.

To make the Aromatic Sambal, heat the oil in a skillet and sauté the Chilli Sambal, Aromatic Nonya Spice Paste and crushed candlenuts or macadamia nuts over medium-low heat for 3–5 minutes until fragrant, making sure the mixture does not burn. Add the dried prawns, tamarind juice and tomato ketchup and cook for about 5 minutes. Season with the lime juice, sugar and salt to taste and cook for 1 more minute. Stir in the coconut cream, mix well and remove from the heat. Transfer the Aromatic Sambal to a serving bowl. Serve the fried anchovies or whitebaits with the bowl of Aromatic Sambal on the side.

SERVES: *4*   **PREPARATION TIME:** *20 mins*   **COOKING TIME:** *15 mins*

250 g (2 cups) dried baby anchovies (*Ikan bilis*) or whitebait, heads and veins removed, rinsed and drained
2 teaspoons rice flour, for dusting
$1^1/_2$ cups (375 ml) oil, to shallow-fry
1–2 teaspoons ground red pepper, or to taste
1 teaspooon thick sweet soy sauce (*kecap manis*)
200 g (1 cup) dry-roasted unsalted peanuts

SUGAR SYRUP
50 g ($^1/_4$ cup) sugar
$^1/_4$ cup (60 ml) water

Sweet and spicy fish nibbles with peanuts

Roasting peanuts have a nutty, caramelised aroma. When combined with fried baby anchovies and then tossed with a sugary syrup, they create a unique aroma. These sugared nibbles go very well with the malty sweetness and floral aromas of beer hops, and are a popular accompaniment to beer served in clubs and good restaurants all over Malaysia and Singapore.

Dust the dried anchovies with the rice flour. Heat the oil in a wok until very hot—it is ready when bubbles form around a skewer dipped in it. Fry the anchovies over medium heat until golden brown and crispy, about 1 minute. Remove them from the oil and drain on paper towels.

Make the Sugar Syrup by combining the sugar and water in a small saucepan over medium heat, stirring until the sugar dissolves. Allow it to boil and simmer uncovered for about 1 minute to thicken the syrup slightly. Remove the Syrup from the heat, pour it into a clean wok and heat over medium heat. When the Sugar Syrup bubbles, add the fried anchovies, ground red pepper and sweet thick soy sauce, and toss well to coat the anchovies with the syrup. Stir in the peanuts and remove from the heat.

SERVES: *4-6*   **PREPARATION TIME:** *30 mins*   **COOKING TIME:** *10 mins*

3 sheets frozen puff pastry (24 cm/9$^{1}/_{2}$ in), thawed
1 egg, beaten

SWEET POTATO FILLING
1 tablespoon oil
2 cloves garlic, minced
$^{1}/_{2}$ tablespoon minced fresh ginger
1 small onion, minced
2 sweet potatoes (300 g/10 oz) peeled and diced to yield 2 cups, then blanched until soft
100 g (1 cup) finely sliced green beans or fresh or frozen green peas
1 tablespoon chopped Vietnamese mint
1$^{1}/_{2}$ tablespoons curry powder
1 cup (250 ml) water
$^{1}/_{2}$ teaspoon ground red pepper (optional)
1 teaspoon sugar
1$^{1}/_{2}$ teaspoons salt

Sweet potato curry puffs

A twist on the familiar vegetarian curry puffs, this great party dish is a pure vegetarian version with rich mint and onion aromas that are released with each bite into a savoury parcel. Serve the puffs with Mint Pachidi Chutney (page 27) if you like.

Prepare the Sweet Potato Filling first by heating the oil in a wok and stir-frying the garlic and ginger over medium heat until fragrant, about 1 minute. Add the onion and stir-fry until transparent. Stir in the blanched sweet potato, green beans or peas, Vietnamese mint and curry powder. Add the water. Cook the ingredients for about 2 minutes, season with the ground red pepper, sugar and salt. Remove from the heat and allow to cool.

Preheat the oven to 180°C (360°F). On a lightly floured work surface, cut each puff pastry sheet into 9 equal squares. To make the puffs, brush two opposite sides of a pastry square with the beaten egg. Place 1$^{1}/_{2}$ tablespoons of the Sweet Potato Filling in the centre of the pastry square and fold the pastry diagonally over the filling, forming a triangle, and then crimp the edges to seal. Place the puff on a baking pan and brush the top with the beaten egg. Continue to make the puffs in the same manner with the remaining ingredients.

Bake the puffs for about 20 minutes until golden and serve immediately.

MAKES: *27 puffs*   **PREPARATION TIME:** *20 mins*   **COOKING TIME:** *40 mins*

Vegetarian fritters with sweet chilli dip

Shallow-fried crispy onions and inviting garlic tease out the flavours in this recipe. You may include anything else your imagination devises, for instance roasted dried prawns, so travel that path for a fragrant result. These simple fritters may be served on their own with a dipping sauce or chopped and add to a summer salad for crisp texture.

1 tablespoon oil
2 cloves garlic, chopped
1 tablespoon finely chopped onion
100 g (²/₃ cup) all-purpose flour
100 g (³/₄ cup) rice flour
Pinch of baking powder
Pinch of salt
Pinch of ground white pepper
1¹/₂ cups (375 ml) water
1 green finger-length chilli, deseeded and
    finely chopped
200 g (1 cup) dried channa dhal (split
    peas), soaked overnight to soften, then
    boiled for 2 hours and drained, or 400 g
    (2 cups) canned garbanzo beans,
    drained and mashed
1 teaspoon cumin seeds, dry-roasted and
    ground, or ¹/₂ teaspoon ground cumin
1 egg, beaten
Oil, for deep-frying

SWEET CHILLI DIP
2 tablespoons Sambal Oelek Chilli Paste
    (page 26) or other sweet chilli paste
1 tablespoon balsamic or Chinese vinegar
1 tablespoon fresh lime juice
2 kaffir lime leaves, minced

Prepare the Sambal Oelek Chilli Paste by following the recipe on page 26.

Prepare the Sweet Chilli Dip first by combining all the ingredients in a bowl and mixing well. Set aside.

Heat the oil in a wok or skillet and sauté the garlic over medium heat until golden brown and fragrant, about 1 minute. Remove from the heat and drain on paper towels. In the same pan, sauté the onion for 1–2 minutes in the same manner.

Sift both types of flour into a mixing bowl. Add the baking powder, salt, pepper and water, and whisk the mixture until smooth. Add the sautéed garlic and onion, and all the other ingredients, except the oil, to the flour mixture and mix well, then leave the batter to stand for 15 minutes.

Heat the oil in a wok or saucepan until very hot. Spoon 1 tablespoon of the batter mixture, roughly shape it into a patty with your fingers and then lower it into the hot oil. Deep-fry the patty for 3–4 minutes, adjusting the heat and constantly turning it, until the fritter is golden brown on all sides. Remove from the oil and drain on paper towels. Continue to deep-fry the rest of the fritters in the same manner. Serve them hot with a bowl of Sweet Chilli Dip on the side.

Note: Instead of using channa dhal or garbanzo beans, substitute 100 g (1 cup) soaked green beans mixed with 200 g (1 cup) mashed potato. You can also add 200 g (1 cup) of fresh prawns or dry-roasted dried prawns in place of the dhal for a non-vegetarian version.

SERVES: *4–6*   PREPARATION TIME: *30 mins*
COOKING TIME: *20 mins*

rice, noodles
and breads

1 fresh chicken (1 kg/2 lbs), with skin on
400 g (2 cups) uncooked long-grain rice,
   washed and drained well
2 star anise pods
2.5 cm (1 in) fresh ginger, peeled and sliced
6 cloves garlic, peeled
2 teaspoons sesame oil
6 cups (1.5 litres) Chicken Stock (page 30)
3 green onions (scallions)
2 teaspoons preserved Chinese cabbage
   (*tang chye*), plus 1 more tablespoon for
   the soup
Salt and ground white pepper, to taste
1 teaspoon sesame oil, to rub into the
   chicken
Thick dark soy sauce

GARLIC GINGER MIX
4 cloves garlic, peeled
2.5 cm (1 in) fresh ginger, peeled and sliced

GARLIC CHILLI SAUCE
$1/4$ cup (60 ml) bottled garlic chilli sauce
1 tablespoon vinegar

ACCOMPANIMENTS
Sliced cucumber
Sliced tomatoes (optional)
Sliced red finger-length chillies
Green onion (scallion) strips

Chicken rice with fresh dipping sauces

Lift the lid while cooking and breathe in deeply the tempting aroma, especially if you are using jasmine rice and a full-bodied chicken stock. The brothy chicken aroma is layered into the dish with star anise, ginger and nutty sesame oil when the chicken is served, making it an enticing and satisfying dish for your family or guests.

Prepare the Chicken Stock by following the recipe on page 30.

Clean the chicken well, removing the fat from under the skin and back. Dice the chicken fat and melt it in a skillet over high heat. Pour the chicken fat over the washed rice and mix well.

Grind the star anise, ginger and garlic in a food processor or a mortar until fine. Rub the paste over the entire body of the chicken and inside the body cavity.

Heat the sesame oil in a wok and stir-fry the fat-coated rice over medium heat until fragrant, 3–5 minutes. Set aside.

Bring the Chicken Stock to a boil in a pot. Add the chicken, green onions, preserved Chinese cabbage, salt and pepper. Return to a boil. Reduce the heat to medium and simmer uncovered, skimming off the foam from the stock, until the chicken is just cooked, 3–4 minutes. Remove from the heat. Remove the chicken from the stock and strain the stock, discarding the solids. Rub the sesame oil over the chicken and set aside. Cut the chicken into bite-sized pieces just before serving.

To cook the rice, place the stir-fried rice, $2^{1}/_{2}$ cups (625 ml) of the reserved stock and salt to taste in the rice cooker. The stock should be 2.5–4 cm ($1–1^{1}/_{2}$ in) above the rice level. Switch on the rice cooker and allow to cook. Alternatively, boil in a saucepan for 1–2 minutes, then cover the pan and simmer over low heat for about 20 minutes until all the water has been absorbed and the rice is cooked. Turn off the heat and allow the rice to sit for 5–10 minutes before removing the lid. If desired, add a little sesame oil to the cooked rice, then fluff with a fork to separate the grains before serving.

Prepare the Garlic Ginger Mix by grinding the garlic and ginger to a paste in a mortar. Prepare the Garlic Chilli Sauce by mixing the ingredients together.

To prepare the soup, boil the remaining stock and preserved Chinese cabbage for about 2 minutes. Remove from the heat and ladle into individual serving bowls.

To serve, place the chicken rice on serving plates. Arrange the chicken pieces and Accompaniments on top. Serve immediately with the soup, Garlic Ginger Mix, Garlic Chilli Sauce, green onions and dark soy sauce on the side.

SERVES: *4-6*   PREPARATION TIME: *45 mins*   COOKING TIME: *30 mins*

200 g (1 cup) uncooked short-grain rice
6 cups (1.5 litres) water
1 tablespoon oil
2 cloves garlic, minced
250 g (8 oz) ground pork or 300 g (10 oz)
    white fish fillets, cubed
4 tablespoons chopped Chinese pickled
    mustard greens (*kiam chye*)
1 tablespoon grated fresh young ginger
2 teaspoons soy sauce
Salt, to taste
Sesame oil, to drizzle
2 green onions (scallions), thinly sliced
3 tablespoons preserved Chinese cabbage
    (*tang chye*)
Chopped red bell pepper or dry-roasted dried
    prawns, to serve
Sprigs of coriander leaves (cilantro), to garnish
Ground white pepper, to taste

Chinese rice congee with all the trimmings

Chok (the Cantonese word for rice congee), is the ultimate comfort food cooked by grandmothers for their grandchildren when they start teething, or a dish brought to your bedside when you are down with a heavy cold. The soft rice served with brined mustard green shreds is subtly aromatic on its own and it can be dressed up with the inviting perfumes of fresh ginger, sesame oil and golden-fried garlic.

Wash the rice in a couple of changes of water until the water runs clear (see page 49). Place in a large saucepan with the water and bring to a boil, then simmer half-covered over medium heat for 30–40 minutes, stirring occasionally and topping it up with boiling water as necessary. When the rice is soft and mushy, remove from the heat and set aside.

Heat the oil in a large saucepan and sauté the garlic over medium heat until fragrant and golden, about 1 minute. Add the cooked rice and stir to combine. Add the ground pork or cubed fish in small bits and stir in the pickled vegetable, ginger and soy sauce. Cook the congee for about 5 minutes, stirring from time to time. Season with salt to taste and remove from the heat. Ladle into individual serving bowls, drizzle with sesame oil on top and sprinkle with green onion, preserved Chinese cabbage and chopped bell pepper or dried prawns. Garnish with coriander sprigs. Sprinkle with ground white pepper and serve hot.

Note: Instead of pork, ground chicken also works well with this recipe. If you like, you can roll the ground meat and add it to the porridge in the form of meatballs.

SERVES: *6*   PREPARATION TIME: *20 mins*   COOKING TIME: *45 mins*

Saffron rice with cloves and cashews

The subtle perfume of saffron, crocus stamens is infused into this golden rice dish which is also strengthened by the sweet aroma of cloves. Given their differences, the warm pungency of cloves works well with light saffron to produce an amazingly scented rice dish.

5–10 saffron threads

1 tablespoon warm milk with $^1/_4$ teaspoon ground turmeric added

200 g (1 cup) uncooked Basmati or long-grain rice

1 tablespoon oil

30 g ($^1/_4$ cup) dry-roasted cashew nuts

1 onion, halved and thinly sliced

2 cardamom pods, crushed and peeled

2 cloves, slightly crushed

1 cup (250 ml) coconut milk, mixed with 2 cups (500 ml) water, or 3 cups (750 ml) Chicken Stock (page 30)

$^1/_2$ teaspoon salt, or to taste

SERVES: 4

PREPARATION TIME: 20 mins

COOKING TIME: 20 mins

Prepare the Chicken Stock by following the recipe on page 30.

Place the saffron threads in a small bowl and cover with the warm milk and turmeric mixture. Allow to soak for 10 minutes.

Wash the rice in a container by covering it with cold water and stirring it, then draining off the water. Repeat this several times until the water drains clear (this removes some of the starch from the rice). Set aside.

Heat the oil in a large skillet and sauté the cashew nuts over medium heat until golden, 1–2 minutes. Turn off the heat and remove the nuts from the skillet, leaving the oil.

Reheat the oil and sauté the sliced onion, cardamom and cloves over medium heat until fragrant, 1–2 minutes. Add the rice and toss for about 5 minutes, until the rice grains become opaque. Remove from the heat and transfer the rice mixture to a large saucepan. Pour in the diluted coconut milk or Chicken Stock until the level is 4 cm ($1^1/_2$ in) above the rice. Stir in the saffron threads with milk and add the salt.

Cook the rice half-covered over medium-high heat until all the liquid is absorbed, 8–10 minutes (cook for a further 3 minutes if the rice is still wet). Reduce the heat to low, cover the pan tightly and turn off the heat. Allow the rice to steam for 10 minutes with the cover on. Fluff the rice with a fork and serve hot with a curry dish.

Fragrant pandanus coconut rice ~ *Nasi lemak*

Creamy and subtle coconut is cooked into my favourite rice dish, *nasi lemak* in Malay, which means rich and creamy rice—which is exactly what it is! When fresh pandanus leaf is added, the special fragrance created is unmatched. Traditionally this rice is served with a hot and spicy prawn or fish sambal and a side dish of cucumber in a banana leaf packet, offering the diner a perfumed surprise when the parcel is unpacked.

400 g (2 cups) uncooked jasmine rice

2 pandanus leaves, tied into a knot, or 2 drops of pandanus essence

3 cups (750 ml) thick coconut milk

1 cup (250 ml) water

1 onion, finely chopped

2 teaspoons salt, or to taste

Place the rice in a container and wash it in a couple of changes of water until the water runs clear, then transfer to a microwave-proof dish.

Add all the other ingredients to the rice and mix well, then cook uncovered in the microwave oven for 20 minutes on high. Alternatively combine all the ingredients in a rice cooker and cook as you would normal rice. Fluff the rice with a fork before serving.

MAKES: 400 g (4 cups)   PREPARATION TIME: 15 mins

COOKING TIME: 20 mins

600 g (1¹/₄ lbs) boneless chicken fillets,
   fat trimmed, sliced into bite-sized chunks
¹/₂ teaspoon salt
¹/₂ tablespoon fresh lime juice
3 tablespoons ghee or butter
2 medium onions, finely sliced
400 g (2 cups) uncooked basmati rice,
   washed and drained, then dried on paper
   towels
5 whole cloves
1 stick cinnamon (8 cm/3¹/₄ in), broken
   into pieces
5 cardamom pods
1 tablespoon minced garlic
1 tablespoon fresh ginger juice (pressed
   from grated fresh ginger)

1 tablespoon Amah's Curry Powder
   (page 62)
¹/₂ tablespoon garam masala
1 tablespoon ground pomegranate seeds
1¹/₂ cups (375 ml) Chicken Stock (page 30)
3 tablespoons plain yoghurt
4-5 saffron threads, soaked in 2 tablespoons
   warm milk
1¹/₂ teaspoons salt
¹/₂ teaspoon ground white pepper
¹/₄ teaspoon rose water (optional)
Sprigs of coriander leaves (cilantro),
   to garnish
Saffron threads, to garnish (optional)

Basmati rice with spiced chicken and yoghurt

Sit back and inhale! This dish is one to be savoured slowly while allowing your senses to separate and identify each aroma and flavour. I normally serve it with a light yoghurt raita and a light vegetarian korma so that the scents do not run rampant. To prepare this dish, you will need a strong, heavy-based pan where the rice can be sautéed and cooked slowly.

Prepare the Chicken Stock and Amah's Curry Powder by following the recipes on pages 30 and 62.

In a bowl, combine the chicken pieces with the salt and lime juice and mix well, then marinate for 10 minutes. Rinse the chicken and drain.

Heat 1 tablespoon of the ghee or butter in a large skillet and sauté half of the onion slices over medium heat until golden brown, 1–2 minutes. Add the rice and half of each of the spices and stir until fragrant, 1–2 minutes. Remove from the heat and cool.

Heat the remaining ghee or butter in a large heavy-based saucepan and sauté the remaining onion slices over medium heat until golden brown, 1–2 minutes. Add the garlic and ginger juice and sauté for 30 seconds, then stir in the remaining spices and mix until fragrant. Add the chicken pieces, Amah's Curry Powder, garam masala, ground pomegranate seeds, mix well and cook for 1–2 minutes. Remove from the heat.

In a bowl, combine the Chicken Stock, yoghurt, saffron and milk, mix well and season with the salt and pepper.

Layer the spiced rice and a layer of the chicken in the bottom of a rice cooker. Continue placing more layers of rice and chicken until they have been used up. Slowly pour in the Chicken Stock mixture until it is about 5 cm (2 in) above the level of the rice or chicken, then gently stir in the rose water (if using). Cover and cook as you would normal rice.

If using a pot to cook the rice, lay the ingredients in the pot in the same manner and cover tightly. Cook over medium heat for about 10 minutes until all the liquid has evaporated, then reduce the heat to low and simmer for 5 more minutes. Remove from the heat. Spoon the spiced chicken rice onto individual serving plates, garnish with coriander leaves and saffron if desired, and serve immediately.

SERVES: *6*   PREPARATION TIME: *45 mins*   COOKING TIME: *30 mins*

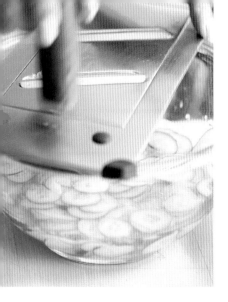

400 g (4 cups) cooked rice

3–4 betel leaves, soaked in water (enough to cover) mixed with 1 tablespoon sugar for 2 hours, then drained and thinly shredded

1 onion, finely sliced and stir-fried until golden in 1 tablespoon oil

60 g ($\frac{1}{2}$ cup) dried prawns, rinsed and dry-roasted until crisp

$\frac{1}{2}$ turmeric leaf, rolled and thinly sliced

2 sprigs curry leaves, chopped

3 sprigs Vietnamese mint, chopped

40 g (1 cup) Thai basil leaves, chopped

40 g (1 cup) mint leaves, chopped

2 kaffir lime leaves, cut into fine threads

1 small sprig fresh thyme, chopped

$\frac{1}{2}$ tablespoon grated fresh galangal root

250 g (1 cup) grated green papaya

10 peppercorns, dry-roasted and crushed

2 tablespoons tamarind pulp, mashed with 4 tablespoons boiling water and strained to obtain the juice

Salt, to taste

PICKLED CUCUMBER

4 baby or Lebanese cucumbers

$\frac{1}{2}$ teaspoon salt

1 cup (250 ml) vinegar

2 tablespoons sugar

Rice salad perfumed with herbs ~ *Nasi ulam*

This rice dish originates from the east coast of Malaysia where it is served cold during the fasting month by the Muslims. The fast is broken with a sweet rosewater drink to slake the thirst, followed by this aromatic herbal rice, searingly hot and tart with fresh lime juice, with a spicy sweet sambal on the side. Herbal rice is said to aid digestion, cleanse and refresh the body. It is served in many parts of Asia, including Myanmar and Indonesia. The Indians serve a similar Ayurvedic-influenced tamarind rice salad believed to "cool" the body.

Prepare the Pickled Cucumber first by thinly slicing the cucumbers with a mandolin as shown. In a large bowl, mix the cucumber slices with a little salt and set aside for 5 minutes. Squeeze the liquid from the cucumber slices, then rinse quickly, drain and dry on paper towels. Combine the vinegar and sugar in a bowl and mix until the sugar is dissolved. Add the sliced cucumber and mix until well coated. Allow to marinate for 2 hours, then drain and set aside.

In a large bowl, combined the cooked rice with all the other ingredients except the tamarind juice and salt. Gently toss the mixture until well blended, adding the tamarind juice a little at a time. Do not use all the tamarind juice; add just enough to separate the rice grains. Season with salt to taste, transfer to a serving platter and serve immediately with the Pickled Cucumber on the side. This dish goes well with pickled limes too.

SERVES: *4–6*   PREPARATION TIME: *45 mins + 2 hours to marinate*   COOKING TIME: *5 mins*

1 lb (500 g) fresh rice stick noodles,
  or 8 oz (250 g) dried rice stick noodles
4 dried sweet Chinese sausages (*lap cheong*),
  finely sliced
8–10 fresh medium prawns (150 g/5 oz),
  peeled and deveined, or freshly shucked
  cockles or oysters
4 cloves garlic, finely chopped
1 tablespoon salted black beans, mashed
  with the back of a spoon
2 tablespoons Sambal Oelek Chilli Paste
  (page 26) or other sweet chilli paste
$1/2$ teaspoon dried prawn paste (*belachan*),
  dry-roasted and crumbled
3 tablespoons thick sweet soy sauce
  (*kecap manis*)
1 tablespoon soy sauce
$1/4$ cup (60 ml) water or as needed
1 bunch garlic chives (about 30), washed
  and cut into short lengths
150 g (3 cups) fresh bean sprouts, trimmed
Fresh lime juice, to taste
Pinch of salt, to taste
Pinch of ground white pepper, to taste

CRISPY PORK CRACKLINGS
50 g ($1/4$ cup) diced pork fat
1 tablespoon water

Bean sauce noodles with prawns and sausage

Char kway teow is a traditional dish that never fails to please with its hot and smoky aromas of spluttering pork fat deliciously browned in spicy black bean sauce. And when the rice noodles and emerald garlic chives are finally thrown in and tossed with the glistening dark sweet soy, the scents are complete in a dish with memorable aromas that linger long after the taste.

Prepare the Crispy Pork Cracklings first. Heat a skillet until hot and sauté the pork fat for 2 minutes, then pour in the water and let it sizzle. As the water evaporates, the fat is rendered. Continue stirring until the pork fat becomes golden and crispy. Turn off the heat, transfer the cracklings to a platter and reserve the oil for stir-frying the noodles.

If using dried rice stick noodles, half-fill a saucepan with water and bring to a boil, then cook the rice noodles for 2–3 minutes until soft. Remove from the heat and drain well.

Heat 2 tablespoons of the pork oil in a deep wok and stir-fry the sausages and prawns over medium heat for 1 minute. Move the sausages and prawns to the sides of the wok to make a well in the centre, add the garlic and stir-fry for 30 seconds until fragrant, then add the black beans, chilli paste and dried prawn paste, and continue to stir-fry for 1 more minute. Combine all the ingredients in the wok and mix well. Add the noodles, a little at a time, and toss well. Drizzle in both soy sauces and toss until the noodles are coated evenly with the sauce—you may need to add a little water to mix the sauces evenly. Finally stir in the chives, bean sprouts, Crispy Pork Cracklings, lime juice, salt and pepper to taste and toss well. Remove from the heat, transfer to individual serving plates and serve immediately.

SERVES: *4-6*   PREPARATION TIME: *30 mins*   COOKING TIME: *10 mins*

½ cup (125 ml) oil
300 g (10 oz) dried rice stick noodles, blanched in boiling water until soft, then drained well
2 eggs, slightly beaten
1 onion, finely chopped
5 cloves garlic, minced
200 g (7 oz) lean pork, thinly sliced and marinated with 1 tablespoon oyster sauce
2 tablespoons dried prawn paste (*belachan*), dry-roasted and crumbled
1 cake pressed firm tofu (150 g/5 oz), diced
1 red finger-length chilli, chopped
2 tablespoons dry-roasted unsalted peanuts, crushed
2 tablespoons chopped coriander leaves (cilantro)
30 g (¾ cup) chopped garlic chives
25 g (½ cup) fresh bean sprouts, tails trimmed
Lime wedges, to garnish

SWEET CHILLI DRESSING
¼ cup (60 ml) fresh lime juice
¼ cup (60 ml) fish sauce
2 tablespoons shaved palm sugar or dark brown sugar, with 4 tablespoons water
1 tablespoon bottled sweet chilli sauce

Rice noodles with pork and sweet chilli dressing

Fresh, wild and wonderful—this dish creates a culinary insurrection on your palate with its unbeatable combination of garlic chives, bean sprouts and coriander leaves, all of which serve to jog your aromatic memory. My friend Simon Goh of Chinta Ria adds a mean chilli dressing when he tosses this particular dish as it is cooked in our hometown of Klang. If dried prawn paste is not your thing, omit it for it might change your appreciation of this vibrant noodle dish. Glasses of beer, aromatic and floral when chilled, go well with this dish.

Heat the oil in a wok and fry the noodles over medium heat for 1–2 minutes until slightly browned. Remove from the pan and drain on paper towels.

Heat 1 tablespoon of the oil in a skillet until hot. Add the beaten egg, swirling the pan to form a thin omelette. Cook the egg until set. Remove from the heat and set aside to cool. Roll up the omelette and slice into thin shreds.

Heat 1 tablespoon of the oil in a wok over high heat and stir-fry the onion and garlic until golden brown and fragrant, about 30 seconds. Add the pork and stir-fry until cooked, 2–3 minutes. Add the dried prawn paste, tofu and chilli, and mix well. Remove from the heat.

Make the Sweet Chilli Dressing by combining all the ingredients in a bowl and mixing well.

In a large serving platter, combine all the ingredients except the egg and lime wedges. Pour the Sweet Chilli Dressing over the noodles and toss until well blended. Sprinkle the egg shreds on top and serve with lime wedges.

SERVES: *4–6*   PREPARATION TIME: *45 mins*   COOKING TIME: *10 mins*

2 cups (500 ml) coconut cream
3 cups (750 ml) water
250 g (1¹/₂ cups) plain flour, sifted
4 eggs, lightly beaten
1¹/₂ teaspoons salt
3 tablespoons oil
1 *roti jala* cup, or empty can with very fine
  holes punched in at the base

Lacy malay coconut pancakes ~ *Roti jala*

These lacy pancakes (the name literally means "fish net bread") are made by pouring a coconut pancake mixture through a can with very fine holes at the base to create whirls of thin batter. A little scent of the coconut remains to intrigue when these interesting net-like pancakes are cooked. It is simple enough for a child to do, as my grandson Isaac has demonstrated.

Dilute the coconut cream with the water in a large bowl and mix well. Place the flour separately in a mixing bowl and gradually pour in the diluted coconut cream, mixing well to form a smooth batter. Strain the batter through a sieve, discarding the solids, then add the beaten egg and salt and strain again.

Grease a non-stick griddle and heat over medium heat. Holding the cup or can over the griddle, pour ¹/₂ cup (125 ml) of the batter into it. As the streams of batter flow onto the griddle, move the cup or can in a circular motion to create a lacy pattern. Cook the pancake on one side for about 2 minutes, then turn it over to cook the other side for 1 minute. Remove from the heat. Continue to make the lacy pancakes in the same manner with the remaining batter. Serve the pancakes with Amah's Aromatic Chicken Curry (page 62). They are just as delicious with maple syrup or honey for breakfast, or as a dessert.

SERVES: *6*   PREPARATION TIME: *10 mins*   COOKING TIME: *15 mins*

1 Pierce fine holes in the bottom of the can.

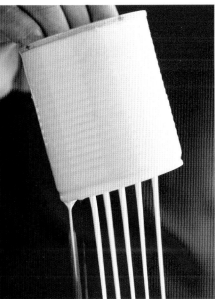

2 Drip streams of batter onto the griddle using the can.

3 Cook the lacy pancake on both sides.

poultry and
meat dishes

500 g (1 lb) boneless chicken thighs, trimmed
75 g ($^1/_2$ cup) all-purpose flour
30 g ($^1/_2$ cup) breadcrumbs
Oil, for deep-frying
$^1/_2$ onion, chopped
2 cloves garlic, minced
150 g (5 oz) fresh shiitake mushrooms, stems trimmed, caps sliced (optional)
1 stalk lemongrass, thick bottom part only, outer layers discarded, inner part sliced and ground in a mortar
$^1/_2$ tablespoon Sambal Oelek Chilli Paste (page 26) or other sweet chilli paste
1 tablespoon brown bean paste (*taucheo*)
1 tablespoon thick sweet soy sauce (*kecap manis*)
$^1/_2$ tablespoon Chinese rice wine
$^1/_2$ tablespoon bottled sweet chilli sauce
1 tablespoon sugar
1 tablespoon fresh lime juice
Salt and ground white pepper, to taste
1 red finger-length chilli, deseeded and sliced, to garnish
Green Onion Curls (page 30), to garnish

MARINADE
$^1/_4$ cup (60 ml) Chinese rice wine
$^1/_4$ cup (60 ml) Chinese black vinegar
2 teaspoons sesame oil
1 tablespoon soy sauce

Sweet soy and sambal fried chicken

The quintessential dish of the Nonyas of Malacca, where each dish is given as much attention as the cook can spare to prepare a percussion of spice and herbal aromas overlain with contrasting tastes and textures.

Prepare the Sambal Oelek Chilli Paste and Green Onion Curls by following the recipes on page 26 and 30.

Combine the Marinade ingredients in a large bowl and mix well. Add the chicken and mix until well coated. Cover and refrigerate for 3–4 hours, then drain. Combine the flour and breadcrumbs in a zip-lock bag. In batches, place the chicken in the flour mixture, shaking the bag to coat them well with the mixture on all sides. Remove from the bag and set aside on a platter.

Heat the oil in a wok and deep-fry the chicken over medium heat for about 1 minute on each side. Remove from the hot oil and drain on paper towels.

Drain off all but 2 tablespoons of the oil in the wok and stir-fry the onion and garlic until fragrant, about 1 minute. Add the mushroom slices (if using) and stir-fry for 1 minute. Stir in the lemongrass, Sambal Oelek Chilli Paste and bean paste and mix well. Return the deep-fried chicken to the wok and stir-fry for 1–2 minutes. Season with the soy sauce, rice wine, sweet chilli sauce, sugar and lime juice, and stir-fry for 1 more minute. Add salt and pepper to taste and remove from the heat. Transfer to a serving platter, garnish with red chilli slices and Green Onion Curls and serve hot.

SERVES: *4–6*   PREPARATION TIME: *30 mins + 3 hours to marinate*   COOKING TIME: *15 mins*

2 tablespoons olive oil

1 kg (2 lbs) store-bought roasted chicken, cut into bite-sized pieces

250 g (8 oz) streaky smoked pork or bacon, cut into chunks

1 large onion, cut into chunks

$1/2$ cup (125 ml) Sambal Oelek Chilli Paste (page 26) or other sweet chilli paste

$1/2$ tablespoon thick sweet soy sauce (*kecap manis*)

1 tablespoon soy sauce

1 tablespoon tomato paste

3 potatoes, peeled and parboiled, then drained and sliced into chunks

Fresh juice of 1 lime

Quick eurasian curry captain

Savour the mouth-watering European and Asian aromas in this dish of roasted chicken and smoked bacon cooked with spicy sweet soy to create an enticing combination of unusual Portuguese Eurasian flavours. This recipe comes from my sister-in-law's family kitchen, where the exploration of aromas and tastes is always invited.

Prepare the Sambal Oelek Chilli Paste by following the recipe on page 26.

Heat 1 tablespoon of the olive oil in a wok and stir-fry the chicken and pork over medium-high heat until crisp, 1–2 minutes. Remove from the heat and set aside. Add the remaining oil to the wok and stir-fry the onion and Sambal Oelek Chilli Paste over medium heat for 1–2 minutes until fragrant. Remove from the heat.

Combine all the ingredients, except the lime juice, in a large saucepan or pot and cook over medium heat for 5–10 minutes, stirring from time to time, until the sauce reduces. Season with the lime juice and remove from the heat. Serve immediately with bread and steamed rice.

SERVES: *6–8*   PREPARATION TIME: *20 mins*   COOKING TIME: *15 mins*

3 cloves garlic, peeled
2.5 cm (1 in) fresh ginger, peeled and sliced
2 tablespoons oil
1 onion, finely chopped
1 stalk curry leaves, plucked and minced
1 kg (2 lbs) boneless chicken thigh fillets,
    sliced into bite-sized pieces
2 cups (500 ml) thick coconut milk
6–8 whole curry leaves
1 tablespoon sugar (optional)
1 teaspoon salt, or to taste
$\frac{1}{2}$ teaspoon ground white pepper
Fresh juice of 1 lime

FRIED ONION RINGS
2 tablespoons ghee or butter
2 small onions, thinly sliced into rings

AMAH'S CURRY POWDER
3 tablespoons coriander seeds, dry-roasted
    and ground
1 tablespoon cumin seeds, dry-roasted and
    ground
1 tablespoon ground red pepper
2 teaspoons ground turmeric
2 teaspoons ground white pepper
1 teaspoon ground cassia or cinnamon

Amah's aromatic chicken curry

My Amah or nanny had the uncanny ability to tease the most tantalising aromas from a handful of garlic gently sautéed with golden caramelised onions. She would then brown the chicken in this, smoother it with perfumed herbs and freshly dry-roasted ground coriander and cumin to produce this unforgettable dish, which combines fragrances reminiscent of anise, parsley and lemon.

Prepare the Fried Onion Rings first by heating the ghee in a skillet and sautéing the onion rings over medium heat until golden and crisp, 2–3 minutes. Remove the onions and drain on paper towels.

Grind the garlic and ginger to a smooth paste in a mortar.

Heat the oil in a wok and stir-fry the ground paste and chopped onion until fragrant, 2–3 minutes. Add the minced curry leaf and stir-fry for 1 more minute. Increase the heat to high, add the chicken pieces and stir-fry for 2–3 minutes until the meat changes colour. Add all the Amah's Curry Powder ingredients and stir-fry until well combined. Pour in 1 cup of the coconut milk, cover and simmer for 3–5 minutes.

Stir in the remaining coconut milk, reduce the heat to low and simmer uncovered until the curry has thickened, 3–5 minutes. Add the whole curry leaves and season with sugar (if using), salt and pepper, stirring well to combine. Taste and adjust the seasonings as desired and remove from the heat. Transfer to a serving bowl, top with Fried Onion Rings and drizzle the lime juice over the top. Serve immediately with steamed rice.

SERVES: *6–8*   PREPARATION TIME: *30 mins*   COOKING TIME: *20 mins*

600 g (1$^1/_4$ lbs) boneless chicken thighs,
    fat trimmed, cut in half
1 tablespoon soy sauce
1$^1/_2$ tablespoons oil
3 cloves garlic, minced
1 tablespoon grated fresh ginger
3 green onions (scallions), sliced into short
    lengths
2 tablespoons Chinese rice wine
    (Shaoxing)
10 g ($^1/_4$ cup) dried woodear or cloud ear
    fungus, soaked in hot water until soft,
    hard bits removed, drained well
1 tablespoon hoisin sauce
$^1/_2$ tablespoon thick sweet soy sauce
    (*kecap manis*)
$^1/_2$ teaspoon salt, or to taste
$^1/_4$ teaspoon ground white pepper
Green Onion Curls (page 30), to garnish

TEA FLAVOURED EGGS
12 quail eggs
1 tablespoon tea leaves
Warm water, to cover
1 teaspoon dark soy sauce

Ginger soy chicken with rice wine

The warm fragrance of ginger and freshly sliced green onion, balanced by floral wine and yeasty soy, creates a memorable combination of flavours and scents to entertain the palate.

Make the Green Onion Curls by following the recipe on page 30.

Prepare the Tea Flavoured Eggs first. Place the eggs in a small saucepan and add enough warm water to cover. Add the tea leaves and bring slowly to a boil over medium-low heat, then simmer uncovered for about 5 minutes. Turn off the heat and remove the eggs from the pan. Roll each egg on a flat work surface to crack the shell on all sides, then return to the saucepan with the tea mixture. Add the dark soy sauce, bring the mixture to a boil and simmer over medium-low heat for 3–5 minutes. Turn off the heat, remove the eggs from the pan and plunge them in a bowl of cold water to cool them. Once they are cool, peel the eggs and set aside.

In a large bowl, combine the chicken and soy sauce and mix well. Heat the oil in a wok until smoky and stir-fry the garlic over medium heat until golden and fragrant, about 20 seconds. Stir in the ginger, green onion and rice wine, then add the chicken and stir-fry for 1–2 minutes. Add the fungus, season with the hoisin sauce and thick sweet soy sauce, and stir-fry for about 1 minute to mix well. Add a little water if the dish appears dry. Cover and simmer for 3–5 minutes until the sauce thickens and the chicken is well cooked. Season with salt and pepper to taste and remove from the heat. Transfer to a serving bowl, top with Tea Flavoured Eggs and garnish with Green Onion Curls. Serve immediately with steamed rice or noodles.

SERVES: *6*   **PREPARATION TIME:** *30 mins*   **COOKING TIME:** *20 mins*

1 kg (2 lbs) pork belly or thigh
1 teaspoon coarse sea salt
2 star anise pods, ground
Oil, for brushing
Bottled sweet chilli sauce, to serve

MARINADE
2 tablespoons thick sweet soy sauce
  (*kecap manis*)
1 tablespoon tomato ketchup
2 cloves garlic, minced
2 tablespoons Chinese black vinegar
2 tablespoons plum sauce
1 tablespoon rice wine
2 tablespoons cornstarch
1 tablespoon brown sugar

Crisp barbecued pork marinated in sweet soy

This roast pork (*char siew*) is pure heaven—golden brown with a slight burnt edge and a light aroma of star anise that teases the burnt sugar into the roasting meat. You don't have to be a rocket scientist to recreate this tender and sumptuous dish in your own kitchen. Sliced diagonally into thin wafers and added to noodles, pasta, fried rice or a sandwich, your *char siew* will easily transform a simple meal.

Place the pork in a large bowl, sprinkle with the salt and ground star anise. Rub the mixture into the pork with your fingers. Allow to stand for 2 hours, then pat dry with paper towels. Using a needle, make deep pricks all over the pork.

Combine all the Marinade ingredients in a bowl and mix well, then pour the Marinade over the pork and rub it into the meat. Allow the pork to marinate for 1 hour, brushing with a little oil.

Preheat the oven to 200°C (400°F). Place the marinated pork in a baking dish and bake in the oven for 15 minutes. Remove the pork from the oven, drain and reserve the liquid collected in the pan. Reduce the temperature to 170°C (340°F) and return the pork to bake for another 10 minutes. Remove from the oven.

Brush the pork with a little salt and grill on a preheated pan grill or under a broiler for 3–5 minutes until crisp, turning often and basting with the reserved liquid. Remove from the heat and cool. Slice the pork thinly and serve with rice, Cabbage Sautéed with Spices (page 92) and a bowl of sweet chilli sauce on the side.

SERVES: *6*   PREPARATION TIME: *20 mins + 3 hours to stand*   COOKING TIME: *30 mins*

1 fresh duck (about 1.5 kg/3 lbs)
2 teaspoons Chinese rice wine
1 teaspoon oil
5 cm (2 in) fresh galangal root (blue ginger), peeled and thinly sliced
10 Asian shallots, peeled but left whole
50 g ($^1/_4$ cup) crushed raw rock sugar
1 stick cinnamon (about 8 cm/3$^1/_4$ in)
2 star anise pods
6 cloves
1 tablespoon dark soy sauce

Sweet blue ginger duck with star anise

This is one of my favourite aromatic recipes for duck. It is heady with the aromas of star anise, cinnamon and the clean fresh fragrance of galangal that not only adds fragrance, but also tenderises the meat until succulent—a recipe from my friend, Pauline Loh.

Clean the duck and rinse well. Trim off the neck, wing tips, tail and webs. Sprinkle the duck with the Chinese rice wine and rub well over the entire body including the cavity. Set aside.

Heat the oil in a wok and stir-fry the galangal slices and whole shallots over medium heat until browned and fragrant, 1–2 minutes. Add the rock sugar and spices and stir until the sugar melts and begins to caramelise.

Place the whole duck in the wok, increase the heat to high and brown the duck on all sides for about 2 minutes, turning the duck using 2 spatulas. Add the dark soy sauce and pour in enough water to cover the duck halfway.

Cook the duck for 30–40 minutes, turning it often. The shallots will melt and thicken the sauce while the duck is cooking. Reduce the heat to low, turn the duck, then cover and simmer for 30 minutes, adding a little water if the duck starts to dry out. Cook uncovered for another 15 minutes and remove from the heat. Remove the duck from the wok and slice into bite-sized pieces, then transfer to a serving platter. Skim off the fat from the surface of the duck gravy and transfer to a serving bowl. Spoon some duck gravy over the duck pieces and serve with steamed rice and the duck gravy on the side.

SERVES: *6*　　PREPARATION TIME: *15 mins*　　COOKING TIME: *1 hour 30 mins*

Beef and mushrooms with chinese broccoli

The success of this recipe relies on the marination of the meat in fragrant mirin, which evaporates when the dish is stir-fried, leaving a wonderful aroma to beguile the senses. Give the wolfberries a try—they give the dish a slight sweetness and add a celebratory touch of red.

350 g (12 oz) beef tenderloin, thinly sliced
1 tablespoon oil
3 cloves garlic, minced
2 tablespoons Chicken Stock (page 30), or water
1 bunch (250 g/8 oz) Chinese broccoli (*kailan*), stems trimmed
5 dried black Chinese mushrooms, soaked in hot water until soft, drained, stems trimmed
1 tablespoon dried Chinese wolfberries or 5 dried Chinese red dates, rinsed
1 teaspoon freshly ground black pepper
1 red finger-length chilli, deseeded and sliced, to garnish

MARINADE
1–2 tablespoons mirin (or rice wine with some sugar added)
$^1/_2$ tablespoon mushroom oyster sauce
$^1/_2$ tablespoon soy sauce

Combine all the Marinade ingredients in a large bowl and mix well. Add the beef strips and mix until well coated. Allow the meat to marinate for at least 2 hours or overnight if possible. Drain the beef and reserve the Marinade.

Heat the oil in a wok and stir-fry the garlic over high heat until golden and fragrant, about 30 seconds. Add the marinated beef strips, toss for 1 minute and remove from the heat. Keep warm.

Add the reserved Marinade and all the other ingredients, except the black pepper and chilli, to the wok and bring to a boil over high heat. Reduce the heat to a simmer, cover and cook for about 1 minute. Season with the pepper and turn off the heat. Return the beef strips to the wok and mix well. Transfer to a serving platter, garnish with the sliced chilli and serve immediately with steamed rice.

SERVES: *4–6*   PREPARATION TIME: *20 mins + 2 hours to marinate*
COOKING TIME: *5 mins*

Grilled beef steak with Malaysian spices

Maximum flavour with minimum fuss, this recipe is guaranteed for success as long as good quality tenderloin is well marinated, grilled quickly and sliced across the grain. Cooked this way, beef is the consummate meal that satisfies.

2 tablespoons fresh lime juice
2 tablespoons soy sauce
700 g (1$^1/_2$ lbs) beef tenderloin
1 tablespoon cumin seeds, dry-roasted and coarsely ground in a mortar
2 teaspoons coriander seeds, dry-roasted and ground in a mortar
1$^1/_2$ teaspoons salt
1 tablespoon oil
Fresh juice of $^1/_2$ lime

Combine the lime juice and soy sauce, then pour this over the beef and coat well with the mixture. Allow to marinate for at least 20 minutes.

Mix the cumin, coriander and salt in a small bowl and rub the mixture into both sides of the beef. Lightly brush with oil and grill the beef on a preheated pan grill or under a broiler for about 3 minutes on each side until cooked, turning often. Remove from the heat.

Slice the grilled beef into thick slices. Arrange on a serving platter, sprinkle with lime juice and serve hot with a salad.

SERVES: *4*   PREPARATION TIME: *10 mins*   COOKING TIME: *15 mins*

4–6 dried tofu skin sheets, each 20 cm
  (8 in) square
2 egg whites, for brushing
Oil, for deep-frying

SWEET BLACK SOY DIPPING SAUCE
$^1/_2$ cup (125 ml) bottled sweet chilli sauce
$^1/_4$ cup (60 ml) thick sweet soy sauce
  (kecap manis)
$^1/_4$ cup (60 ml) rice wine
$^1/_2$ tablespoon Chinese black vinegar,
  or to taste

FILLING
250 g (8 oz) ground fatty pork
250 g (8 oz) ground lean pork
6 fresh or canned water chestnuts, peeled
  and finely diced
$^1/_2$ teaspoon ground white pepper
$1^1/_2$ tablespoons sugar
$^1/_2$ tablespoon Sambal Oelek Chilli Paste
  (page 26) or other sweet chilli paste
1 tablespoon dark soy sauce
1 teaspoon hoisin sauce
40 g ($^1/_3$ cup) sticky (glutinous) rice flour

Sausage rolls with sweet soy dip

Loh bak, the tofu skin rolls are one of the classic favourites, containing a rich pork filling blended with sticky sweet hoisin, salty and yeasty dark soy, and crunchy water chestnuts. These rolls create their own flavours and exude a steamy bouquet as they cook in their paper-thin tofu skins. Serve them on their own with a sweet and pungent Chinese vinegar soy dip.

Prepare the Sambal Oelek Chilli Paste by following the recipe on page 26.

Prepare the tofu skin sheets first. Soak 2 clean dish towels in warm water and then squeeze out the water. Lay the damp towels out flat on a work surface and place the tofu skin sheets in between the two towels for about 10 minutes to soften them, then remove them carefully and brush with the egg white. Cover the softened sheets with a damp towel.

Combine all the Sweet Black Soy Dipping Sauce ingredients in a serving bowl and mix well. Set aside

Combine the Filling ingredients in a large bowl and mix well. To make the pork rolls, wet your hands and divide the Filling into 4 equal portions. Roll each portion into a long sausage-like cylinder, about 2.5 cm (1 in) in diameter and 15 cm (6 in) long. Place one portion along one edge of a tofu skin square. Roll the skin around the Filling, then fold in the sides and roll up tightly, dabbing the inside edge with a little water if necessary and pressing to seal. Continue to make the rolls in the same manner with the remaining ingredients. Place the pork rolls in a heatproof dish.

Half-fill a wok with water and bring to a rapid boil. Place the dish with the pork rolls in a bamboo steamer and set the steamer over the boiling water to steam for about 10 minutes. Remove from the heat and set aside to cool.

Heat the oil in a wok and deep-fry the pork rolls, a few at a time and turning them often, over medium heat for 2–3 minutes, until crispy and golden brown on all sides. Remove from the hot oil and drain on paper towels.

Slice each deep-fried roll into several pieces and arrange them on a serving platter. Serve with the serving bowl of Sweet Black Soy Dipping Sauce on the side.

Note: It's a good idea to prepare extra tofu skin sheets in case 1 or 2 of them tears during rolling. You can substitute filo pastry if tofu skin sheets are not available—use 3 filo sheets to make each pork roll. Then bake the rolls instead of steaming and frying them. You will need 12 filo pastry sheets to make this recipe.

SERVES: *6–8*   **PREPARATION TIME:** *1 hour*   **COOKING TIME:** *20 mins*

1 tablespoon oil

6 cloves garlic, bruised

500 g (1 lb) pork belly, skin removed and discarded, cubed

500 g (1 lb) pork ribs or 300 g (10 oz) pork shoulder, sliced into pieces

3 star anise pods, coarsely ground in a mortar

$\frac{1}{2}$ teaspoon Sichuan pepper (optional)

2 tablespoons chilli black bean sauce

2 tablespoons Sambal Oelek Chilli Paste (page 26) or other sweet chilli paste

$\frac{1}{2}$ cup (125 ml) thick sweet soy sauce (kecap manis)

3 cups (750 ml) water

2 teaspoons shaved palm sugar or dark brown sugar

$\frac{3}{8}$ cup (100 ml) sweet Chinese black vinegar

2 tablespoons Chinese rice wine

8 dried black Chinese mushrooms, soaked in hot water until soft, drained and stir-fried in 2 teaspoons of oil for 2–3 minutes

Salt, to taste

Crispy Fried Garlic (page 30), to garnish

Green Onion Curls (page 30), to garnish

SWEET CUCUMBER PICKLES

$\frac{1}{2}$ cup (125 ml) vinegar

2 tablespoons sugar

1 cucumber, halved lengthwise, cored and thinly sliced

Sweet soy pork with mushrooms and star anise

This caramelised pork dish which is known in Malaysia as *Tau Yew Bak* was a speciality of my Cantonese amah who understood that the flavour and aroma that went hand in hand to create it. Over the years I've improved it by adding black bean sauce and chilli and caramelising the pork so that it becomes a dish with an amazing complexity of flavour. Once I had difficulty getting some air tickets for a television program overseas. I invited the manager of an airline company and served him dinner with this dish. We got the tickets. It may be a coincidence, but this dish has always worked its magic at other times and a colleague of mine dubbed it my "lethal weapon." It might bring you success too!

Make the Crispy Fried Garlic and Green Onion Curls by following the recipes on page 30.

Prepare the Sweet Cucumber Pickles by combining the vinegar and sugar in a bowl and stirring until the sugar is dissolved. Add the cucumber slices and mix well. Allow to marinate for 2 hours and drain the pickles just before serving.

Heat the oil in a wok and stir-fry the garlic over high heat until golden and fragrant, about 30 seconds. Add both types of pork, the star anise and Sichuan pepper (if using) and stir-fry for 1–2 minutes. Add the chilli black bean sauce, Sambal Oelek Chilli Paste and thick sweet soy sauce and toss well to coat the pork with the sauce.

Pour in the water and bring the ingredients to a boil. Reduce the heat to medium and simmer covered until the pork is very tender, about 20–30 minutes. Season with the sugar, vinegar and rice wine, and stir in the mushrooms. Half cover the pan and simmer over low heat for 1 hour, until the pork is tender and the sauce is thick but not completely dried up. Increase the heat to medium, season with salt to taste and stir-fry the pork to coat it evenly with the sauce. Remove from the heat.

Transfer the pork to a serving bowl and sprinkle with Crispy Fried Garlic. Garnish with Green Onion Curls and serve immediately with steamed rice and the Sweet Cucumber Pickles on the side.

SERVES: *6–8* **PREPARATION TIME:** *45 mins + marination time* **COOKING TIME:** *1 hour 10 mins*

seafood dishes

3 tablespoons oil
1 onion, sliced
2 tablespoons Lemongrass Paste (page 29)
1–2 tablespoons Sambal Oelek Chilli Paste
  (page 26), or other sweet chilli paste
1 teaspoon dried prawn paste (*belachan*),
  crumbled and dry-roasted
2 tablespoons tamarind pulp, mashed with
  1 cup (250 ml) water and strained to
  obtain the juice
2 tablespoons fresh pineapple juice
2 cups (500 ml) Fish Stock (page 30)
200 g (1$^1/_2$ cups) fresh ripe pineapple
  chunks
1 tablespoon sugar
$^1/_2$ teaspoon salt, or to taste
600 g (1$^1/_4$ lbs) swordfish or mackerel
  fillets, sliced into bite-sized chunks
3 kaffir lime leaves, slice into fine strips,
  to garnish

Fish in sweet and sour pineapple broth

This traditional Malaysian sweet, sour and spicy fish dish (*Ikan asam pedas*) combines the breezy tropics with simple sour and sweet fruity tastes and is best served in summer when the flavours lend themselves to light dinners. Serve it with a light refreshing beer with a slightly bitter aftertaste and lots of fluffy white rice.

Prepare the Sambal Oelek Chilli Paste, Lemongrass Paste and Fish Stock by following the recipes on page 26, 29 and 30.

Heat the oil in a wok and stir-fry the onion, Lemongrass Paste, Sambal Oelek or sweet chilli paste and dried prawn paste over medium heat until fragrant, 2–3 minutes, making sure the mixture doesn't burn. Stir in the tamarind juice, pineapple juice and Fish Stock and bring to a boil, then simmer uncovered for 1 minute. Add the pineapple chunks and continue to simmer over low heat for 10–12 minutes for the flavours to penetrate, then season with the sugar and salt. The soup should be light, not too tart or sweet.

Gently lower the fish pieces into the simmering broth and simmer over medium heat for 3–5 minutes until just cooked, adjusting the seasonings as needed. Remove from the heat, transfer to a serving bowl and garnish with kaffir lime strips on top. Serve immediately with steamed rice or a simple fresh salad.

SERVES: *4-6*   PREPARATION TIME: *20 mins*   COOKING TIME: *15 mins*

2 tablespoons oil
$\frac{1}{4}$ teaspoon fenugreek seeds
5 cloves garlic, chopped
1 onion, chopped
1 stalk curry leaves plucked and chopped
1 green and 1 red finger-length chilli,
   halved and deseeded
3 ripe tomatoes, quartered
2 tablespoons tamarind pulp, mashed with
   1 cup (250 ml) hot water and strained to
   obtain the juice
3 tablespoons Fish Curry Powder (page 29)
One 450-g (16-oz) can sardines in tomato
   sauce
Salt, to taste

Tomato and tamarind fish curry

Surprise your guests with the delicious aroma of fried garlic and onion combined with the sweet lemon-peppery fragrance of curry leaves as you build up this quick and easy curry using canned sardines. Malaysians often keep a can of sardines on standby in case their guests drop in unexpectedly.

Prepare the Fish Curry Powder by following the recipe on page 29.

Heat the oil in a saucepan and sauté the fenugreek seeds for a few seconds. Add the garlic, onion, curry leaves and chillies and sauté until golden and fragrant, about 2 minutes. Stir in the tomato and sauté for 1–2 more minutes.

Pour in the tamarind juice and add the Fish Curry Powder, then cover and bring to a boil. Reduce the heat to low and simmer for 10 minutes. Stir in the sardines and continue to simmer uncovered for 3 more minutes. Season with salt to taste and remove from the heat. Serve immediately with steamed rice.

Note: If you do not wish to make your own Fish Curry Powder, you may purchase the premix curry powder from supermarkets or Indian grocers.

SERVES: *4*   PREPARATION TIME: *20 mins*   COOKING TIME: *20 mins*

2–3 fresh crabs (total of 2 kg/4 lbs)
1 tablespoon oil
1 teaspoon dried prawn paste (*belachan*),
    dry-roasted and crumbled
1 tablespoon brown bean paste (*taucheo*),
    rinsed to remove excess salt, mashed
8 cloves garlic, smashed with a cleaver
1 tablespoon finely grated fresh ginger
2 tablespoons Sambal Oelek Chilli Paste
    (page 26) or other sweet chilli paste
$\frac{1}{2}$ cup (125 ml) boiling water
2 tablespoons Chinese sweet vinegar
2 tablespoons tomato ketchup
2 teaspoons sugar
1 tablespoon cornstarch mixed with $\frac{1}{2}$ cup
    (125 ml) water
$\frac{1}{2}$ teaspoon salt, or to taste
5–8 garlic chives, cut into lengths

Chilli crabs with ginger and garlic chives

Malaysian Chilli Crab is perhaps intimidating to anyone not used to strong flavours. But the combination of bean paste, prawn paste and chilli adds a tantalising aroma to this dish. And diners are beguiled into enjoyment as they taste this extraordinary dish. Chilli crab is best cooked and eaten at home where everyone can relax and enjoy the fun of prying the crabshells with a fork or fingers to get at that final tasty morsel inside.

Prepare the Sambal Oelek Chilli Paste by following the recipe on page 26.

Scrub the crabs thoroughly and rinse well. Detach the claws from each crab and lift off the shell. Scrape out and discard the gills. Quarter each crab with a cleaver and crack the claws with a mallet or nut cracker.

Heat the oil in a wok and stir-fry the dried prawn paste and bean paste over medium heat until fragrant, about 30 seconds, taking care not to burn the mixture. Add the garlic, ginger and Sambal Oelek or sweet chilli paste and stir-fry for 1 minute. Stir in the crab pieces and toss well, then add the boiling water, mixing to coat the crab well with the sauce. Cover and simmer for 3–5 minutes. Season with the vinegar, tomato ketchup and sugar, and simmer for 2 more minutes. Pour in the cornstarch mixture and toss until the sauce thickens and the crab pieces are cooked. Season with salt and remove from the heat. Sprinkle with the garlic chives and serve immediately.

SERVES: *6*   PREPARATION TIME: *30 mins*   COOKING TIME: *15 mins*

1 fresh snapper head (about 500 g/1 lb)
2 tablespoons oil
2 tablespoons Aromatic Nonya Spice Paste
  (page 28)
1 tablespoon Sambal Oelek Chilli Paste
  (page 26) or other sweet chilli paste
  with prawn paste in it
1 tablespoon Fish Curry Powder (page 29)
1 sprig curry leaves (about 15 leaves)
$1/_2$ tablespoon tamarind pulp, mashed with
  $1/_4$ cup (60 ml) hot water and strained to
  obtain the juice
$1^1/_2$ cups (375 ml) water or Fish Stock
  (page 30)
Salt and ground white pepper, to taste

Fish head curry

Heaven to true gastronomes, this blend of perfumed herbs and spices—including citrusy lemongrass, refreshing galangal and mint—adds amazing scents and flavours to the sauce. Fish head curry is prized in Malaysia for the meat around the cheeks and eyes.

Prepare the Sambal Oelek Chilli Paste, Aromatic Nonya Spice Paste, Fish Curry Powder and Fish Stock by following the recipes on pages 26, 28, 29 and 30.

Scale and clean the fish head thoroughly. Cut off the gills with a pair of kitchen scissors. Cut the head into half lengthwise so that the 2 halves can sit flat in the pan. Rinse well, then pat dry with paper towels.

Heat the oil in a wok and stir-fry the Aromatic Nonya Spice Paste, Sambal Oelek, Fish Curry Powder and curry leaves over medium heat until fragrant, about 3 minutes. Stir in the tamarind juice and water or Fish Stock and bring to a boil. Reduce the heat to low, cover and simmer for about 3 minutes or until the curry is slightly thickened.

Add the fish head to the curry, increase the heat to high and bring to a boil, turning the fish a few times to coat it well with the curry. Lower the heat and simmer uncovered for about 3 minutes until the fish is cooked and the curry is thick. Season with salt and pepper to taste, adjusting with more tamarind juice if desired. Remove from the heat and transfer to a large serving bowl. Serve hot with steamed rice, Okra Stuffed with Prawn Sambal (page 94) and a yoghurt raita.

SERVES: *4-6*   PREPARATION TIME: *45 mins*   COOKING TIME: *10 mins*

2 tablespoons oil
2 cloves garlic, minced
$1/2$ tablespoon finely grated fresh ginger
500 g (1 lb) fresh prawns, peeled, with tails
    left on
1 tablespoon vinegar
1 tablespoon soy sauce
1 teaspoon sugar
$1/4$ cup (60 ml) water
1 teaspoon salt, or to taste

GINGER FLOWER SAMBAL
5–8 red finger-length chillies, halved
    lengthwise and deseeded
8 cm ($3^1/4$ in) fresh turmeric root, peeled
    and sliced
10 cm (4 in) fresh galangal root, peeled
    and sliced
5 stalks lemongrass, thick bottom part only,
    outer leaves discarded, inner part sliced
$1/2$ turmeric leaf
1 ginger flower, sliced
10 g ($1/4$ cup) Vietnamese mint
1 pandanus leaf
2 teaspoons dried prawn paste (*belachan*),
    dry-roasted

Amah's fragrant sambal prawns

The ginger flower—with its rose-like pungency of turmeric, spike of ginger and freshness of galangal and lemongrass all rolled into one—is irresistible; something that leaves diners intrigued and returning for more. It is the most beautiful of all herbs, ranging from light to startling bright pink, with petals that appear to fold themselves into a prayerful pose. A sambal or salsa made with this mix of ingredients will create its very own perfume that is unmatched by any other combination of herbs in the Nonya repertoire.

Prepare the Ginger Flower Sambal first by grinding the chillies in a food processor until smooth. Add the rest of the ingredients and continue grinding to a smooth paste. Set aside.

Heat the oil in a wok and stir-fry the garlic and ginger over medium heat until golden, 1–2 minutes. Add the Ginger Flower Sambal and stir-fry until fragrant, about 3 minutes. Stir in the prawns and toss for 1–2 minutes until pink and coated well with the ground paste. Add the vinegar, soy sauce, sugar and water, mix well and simmer uncovered for 1 minute. Season with the salt and remove from the heat. Transfer to a serving platter and serve with steamed rice or a noodle dish.

SERVES: *4–6*   PREPARATION TIME: *40 mins*   COOKING TIME: *10 mins*

3 fresh lobsters (each 500 g/1 lb) or 1.5 kg
   (3 lbs) fresh crayfish
$^1/_2$ cup (125 ml) oil
5 tablespoons butter
7 cloves garlic, crushed
1 teaspoon black peppercorns, coarsely
   cracked in a mortar or spice grinder
1 tablespoon rice vinegar
1 tablespoon sugar
$^1/_2$ teaspoon salt, or to taste
Salmon roe, to garnish

MARINADE
1 teaspoon coarsely ground black
   peppercorns
2 tablespoons soy sauce
$^1/_2$ tablespoon sugar

Black pepper lobster tails with garlic butter

A seafood dish that is a gastronomic delight and a triumph for the cook as the pepper-spiked lobster is lowered into hot butter and tossed quickly. The sweetness of butter and sizzling lobster quickly wafts into the dining room enticing all within reach.

If using live lobsters, freeze them for 1 hour, then lay on the chopping board and cut through the head along the point between the eyes with the back of a cleaver or a sharp knife to quickly kill them. Omit the freezing step if using frozen lobsters. Twist off the claws and detach the tails from the heads by inserting a knife into the gap between the tail and head. Crack the claws with a cracker or hammer, and quarter each lobster tail. Discard the heads. If using crayfish, rinse and scrub them well to remove the mud. Detach the bodies from the heads by twisting off the head of each crayfish. Discard the heads and halve each crayfish. Pat dry the lobster or crayfish pieces with paper towels.

Combine all the Marinade ingredients in a bowl and mix well. Pour the Marinade over the lobster or crayfish pieces and mix until well coated. Allow to marinate for at least 1 hour.

Heat the oil in a wok until hot. In small batches, stir-fry the lobster or crayfish pieces over medium heat until red and crispy, 2–3 minutes. Remove from the heat and drain on paper towels, keeping warm.

In another wok, melt the butter over medium heat and then stir-fry the garlic until golden brown and fragrant, 1–2 minutes. Add the cracked black peppercorns and mix well. Add the fried lobster or crayfish pieces and toss until well coated. Season with the rice vinegar, sugar and salt, and remove from the heat. Transfer to a serving platter and sprinkle with the salmon roe. Serve hot.

SERVES: *4-6*   PREPARATION TIME: *20 mins + 1 hour to marinate*   COOKING TIME: *10 mins*

500 g (1 lb) fresh jumbo prawns
Bamboo skewers (1 for each prawn),
   soaked in water for 1 hour before using
Fresh juice of 1 lime mixed with $\frac{1}{2}$
   teaspoon ground turmeric
Coconut cream and bottled chilli sauce, for
   brushing on the prawns (optional)
Lettuce leaves, to garnish
Lemon wedges, to serve

SPICE PASTE
$\frac{1}{2}$ cup (125 ml) Lemongrass Paste (page 29)
1 teaspoon Sambal Oelek Chilli Paste (page
   26) or other sweet chilli paste (optional)
$\frac{3}{4}$ cup (200 ml) coconut cream
1 tablespoon fish sauce
1 tablespoon shaved palm sugar or dark
   brown sugar
1 tablespoon oil

Grilled prawns with lemongrass

This recipe uses my favourite ingredient—lemongrass—which becomes lightly aromatic when ground and softened by the "coconutty" aroma of palm sugar on beautifully grilled prawns. What better gift for a lover or friend than to prepare these fragrant skewers?

Prepare the Sambal Oelek Chilli Paste and Lemongrass Paste by following the recipes on pages 26 and 29.

Clean and trim the prawns and cut the shells open along their underside. Then thread each one onto a bamboo skewer lengthwise. Place in a large grilling tray and drizzle with the lime and turmeric mixture. Set aside.

Prepare the Spice Paste by combining all the ingredients, except the oil, in a bowl and mixing well. Heat the oil in a skillet and sauté the Spice Paste over medium heat for 3–5 minutes until fragrant. Remove from the heat. Spread the Spice Paste over the skewered prawns and into the underside cavities. Brush with a little coconut cream and chilli sauce if desired. Grill the prawns on a preheated pan grill or under a broiler for about 3 minutes or until cooked, turning often and making sure they do not burn. Arrange the grilled prawns on serving platters lined with lettuce leaves and serve immediately.

SERVES: *4–6*   PREPARATION TIME: *20 mins*   COOKING TIME: *20 mins*

Fresh seafood salad with tangy dressing

Yusheng is a seafood feast lit by sparks of stray light on silky white squid, lime-tinged crystalline prawns and freshly filleted sweet fish—a salty, fresh combination of aromas, colours, textures and flavours. I temper this feast of the senses with a nutty and truffle-like dressing balanced with special Shaoxing rice wine that has the surprising raisin-like perfume of a rich port wine.

6 fresh medium squids (300 g/10 oz total)
300 g (10 oz) fresh sashimi grade fish fillets (salmon, tuna or white fish)
300 g (10 oz) fresh medium prawns, peeled and deveined, tails left on
$1/2$ cup (125 ml) fresh lime juice
100 g (1 cup) snowpeas, trimmed and sliced in half lengthwise
10 asparagus spears, tough ends trimmed
1 stalk celery, thinly sliced diagonally
1 red bell pepper, cut in half, cored, deseeded and sliced
20 g ($1/2$ cup) dried woodear or cloud ear fungus, soaked in hot water until soft, hard bits trimmed, drained well
1 teaspoon grated lime rind

SESAME LIME DRESSING
$3/4$ cup (200 ml) Chicken Stock (page 30)
2 tablespoons Shaoxing rice wine
1 tablespoon fine granulated sugar
$1^1/_2$ teaspoons sesame oil
1 tablespoon oyster or mushroom oyster sauce
2 teaspoons Worcestershire sauce
1 teaspoon fresh lime juice
$1/2$ teaspoon salt, or to taste
$1/4$ teaspoon ground white pepper

DIPPING SAUCE
$1/4$ cup (60 ml) fresh lime juice
1 teaspoon sugar
1 teaspoon bottled sweet chilli sauce
2 kaffir lime leaves, cut into thin shreds

SERVES: *6*

PREPARATION TIME: *1 hour 30 mins*

COOKING TIME: *5 mins*

Prepare the Chicken Stock by following the recipe on page 30.

Rinse the squids, pull the heads and innards from the tubelike bodies. Discard the heads but retain the tentacles, and remove the beak from the mouth. Clean the body tubes, removing and discarding the long, thin cartilage inside. Halve each tube lengthwise and rinse the inside well. Using a sharp knife, score the flesh on the inside by making diagonal criss-cross slits across the surface, then slice into bite-sized pieces. Half-fill a saucepan with water and bring to a boil. Poach the squid pieces in the boiling water for about 1 minute, then remove and immediately plunge into a bowl of iced water to stop the cooking process. Set aside.

Place the fish fillets and prawns in a bowl and pour the lime juice over them. Refrigerate for 15 minutes, turning over once. Remove from the refrigerator and drain off the lime juice. Slice the fish fillets into bite-sized strips. Place all the seafood in a platter and refrigerate until ready to serve.

Half-fill a saucepan with water and bring to a boil. Blanch the snowpeas and asparagus separately for about 1 minute each. Remove from the heat and immediately plunge into iced water to stop the cooking process. Drain well and refrigerate together with the other vegetables, until ready to serve.

To prepare the Sesame Lime Dressing, combine all the ingredients in a bowl and mix well.

Make the Dipping Sauce by mixing all the ingredients until the sugar is dissolved. Divide into several tiny dipping bowls.

To serve, arrange the seafood and vegetables on a large platter and scatter the grated lime rind over the fish pieces. Place the platter with the bowl of Sesame Lime Dressing in the centre of the dining table and tiny bowls of Dipping Sauce around them. Provide each guest with a pair of chopsticks and a small side plate. Begin by pouring the Sesame Lime Dressing over the salad, then invite your guests to toss the ingredients all at once using their chopsticks for health and prosperity.

1 kg (2 lbs) white fish fillets, sliced into
    5-cm (2-in) chunks
$\frac{1}{2}$ teaspoon ground turmeric
Twelve 20-cm (8-in) banana leaf squares,
    blanched in boiling water to soften
$\frac{1}{2}$ cup (125 ml) fresh lime juice
Toothpicks, to fasten
1 tablespoon ghee or melted butter mixed
    with 1 tablespoon oil
Chopped red finger-length chillies, to
    garnish
Mint leaves, to garnish

COCONUT AND GREEN MANGO PASTE
250 g ($2\frac{1}{2}$ cups) freshly grated coconut or
    150 g (1 cup) dried unsweetened grated
    (desiccated) coconut
3–4 green finger-length chillies, halved and
    deseeded
40 g (1 cup) coriander leaves (cilantro)
8 cloves garlic, peeled
2 teaspoons ground cumin, dry-roasted
$\frac{1}{2}$ teaspoon sugar, or to taste
1 teaspoon salt, or to taste
1 green mango (about 150 g/5 oz), peeled
    and pitted, flesh cut into thin strips
1 tablespoon ghee or melted butter mixed
    with 1 tablespoon oil

Grilled green mango fish parcels

This recipe is one of my favourite for it shows off fish in an aromatic and beautiful way. I first tasted it in Mumbai at a food writer's home and I can never forget the experience. Whiting is a good fish to use in this recipe if you do not mind the bones, as it cooks fast and has the most tender and sweet flesh. Bream, mackerel or any other firm white fish works just as well.

Wash the fish fillets and pat dry with paper towels. Place in a large bowl with the ground turmeric and mix until well coated. Set aside.

Prepare the Coconut and Green Mango Paste by processing the grated coconut in a food processor until fine. Add the chilli, coriander leaves and garlic, and process to a smooth paste. Transfer to a bowl and stir in the cumin, sugar, salt and mango strips. Heat the ghee and oil in a nonstick skillet and sauté the ground mixture over medium heat until fragrant, 2–3 minutes. Remove from the heat and set aside.

Divide the fish into 12 equal portions. Place a portion of the fish in the centre of a banana leaf square, coat it with the Coconut and Green Mango Paste on all sides and sprinkle lime juice on top. Fold the banana leaf up into a parcel and secure the open side with a toothpick. Continue to make the other fish parcels in the same manner with the remaining ingredients.

Heat the ghee and oil in a large skillet over medium heat. Handling 2 parcels at a time, fry the parcels over medium heat for about 3 minutes on each side, until the fish is cooked. Alternatively, bake the parcels in a preheated oven at 170°C (340°F) for 25 minutes in a fan forced oven. Remove from the heat, unwrap the parcels and serve hot with saffron or coconut rice, garnished with chopped chilli and mint leaves.

MAKES: *12 parcels*   **PREPARATION:** *45 mins*   **COOKING:** *25 mins*

vegetable dishes

3 tablespoons oil
100 g (1 cup) diced tempeh
2 tablespoons Lemongrass Paste (page 29)
2 medium onions, finely chopped
3 cloves garlic, finely chopped
1 tablespoon Sambal Oelek Chilli Paste
   (page 26) or other sweet chilli paste
350 g (12 oz) green beans, trimmed ad
   sliced diagonally to make 3 cups
1 teaspoon brown sugar, or to taste
2 bay leaves
$1/2$–1 cup (125 ml–250 ml) thick coconut
   milk
1 teaspoon salt, or to taste
1 tablespoon fresh lemon juice

Sambal tempeh and green beans

A fragrant crunchy vegetarian dish that may be enjoyed with rice or tossed with noodles.

Prepare the Sambal Oelek Chilli Paste and Lemongrass Paste by following the recipes on pages 26 and 29.

Heat 2 tablespoons of the oil in a wok and fry the tempeh cubes over medium heat until crisp, about 2 minutes. Remove from the heat and drain on paper towels.

Wipe the wok clean and heat the remaining oil, then stir-fry the Lemongrass Paste, onion, garlic and Sambal Oelek over high heat until aromatic, 1–2 minutes. Add the green beans and fried tempeh and stir-fry for 2–3 minutes until the vegetable is tender. Add the brown sugar and toss well. Add the bay leaves and the coconut milk, reduce the heat to low and simmer uncovered until the sauce thickens, 3–5 minutes. Season with salt and removed from the heat, then stir in the lemon juice. Serve hot as part of a rice meal.

Note: Always remove the pan from the heat before adding the lemon juice to the coconut milk, or it will separate and curdle.

SERVES: *4-6*   PREPARATION TIME: *20 mins + time to prepare Lemongrass Paste*   COOKING TIME: *10 mins*

3 tablespoons oil
200 g (2 cups) diced tempeh
$^1/_2$ onion, thinly sliced
1 clove garlic, minced
1 stalk lemongrass, thick bottom part only,
    outer leaves discarded, inner part sliced
    and ground in a mortar
$^1/_2$ teaspoon ground red pepper
$^1/_2$ teaspoon dried prawn paste (*belachan*),
    dry-roasted
$1^1/_2$ tablespoons shaved palm sugar or dark
    brown sugar
$^1/_4$ cup (60 ml) water
Fresh juice of $^1/_2$ lemon
Salt and ground white pepper, to taste
100 g (1 cup) snowpeas, trimmed and
    blanched for 2 minutes (optional)
3 kaffir lime leaves, sliced into thin shreds

Tempeh with snowpeas

A form of cultured soybeans similar to tofu, the smoky-tasting tempeh has more protein and textural flavour than normal tofu. With a blend of lemongrass, dried prawn paste and sugar that reminds you of the sweet aromas of laksa, this delicious sambal provides both taste and health.

Heat 2 tablespoons of the oil in a wok and fry the tempeh cubes over medium heat until crisp, about 2 minutes. Remove from the heat and drain on paper towels.

Wipe the wok clean, then heat the remaining oil and stir-fry the onion and garlic over high heat until golden and tender, about 1 minute. Add the lemongrass, ground red pepper, dried prawn paste, sugar and 3 tablespoons of the water and stir-fry for 2 minutes. Reduce the heat to medium and continue to stir-fry the ingredients until they caramelise.

Return the fried tempeh to the wok and toss until well coated with the caramelised spices, adding more water as necessary. Season with the lemon juice and salt and pepper to taste. Remove from the heat. Arrange the snowpeas (if using) on a serving platter and place the cooked tempeh on top. Sprinkle with the kaffir lime leaf shreds and serve hot.

SERVES: *4*   PREPARATION TIME: *30 mins*   COOKING TIME: *10 mins*

1 tablespoon oil
1 teaspoon black mustard seeds
2 cloves garlic, chopped
1 large onion, halved and finely sliced
500 g (4 cups) thinly sliced cabbage
Pinch of ground turmeric
2 eggs, beaten
1 teaspoon salt, or to taste
$^1/_2$ teapoon ground white pepper
6–8 curry leaves, chopped

Cabbage sautéed with spices

This is an ideal recipe to dress up plain tasting cabbage. Nose-spiking mustard seeds combine with the aromas of onion, garlic and curry leaves to spice up the dish. This cabbage dish has been cooked in our home for as long as I can remember, and is as surprising as it is tasty. This dish goes well with any of the fish curries in this book.

Heat the oil in a wok and fry the mustard seeds over high heat until they pop. Add the garlic and onion and stir-fry until golden and tender, about 2 minutes. Stir in the cabbage and ground turmeric, and toss well. Reduce the heat to a simmer, cover and cook for 3–5 minutes, stirring occasionally.

Remove the cover, push the cabbage to the sides of the wok to make a well in the centre and pour in the beaten egg. Cook the eggs until set, then scramble gently and toss with the cabbage until well blended. Season with salt and pepper, adjusting the taste. Stir in the curry leaves and remove from the heat. Serve immediately with steamed rice.

SERVES: *4-6*   PREPARATION TIME: *20 mins*   COOKING TIME: *10 mins*

¼ cup (60 ml) oil
50 g (½ cup) diced dried salted fish
   (preferably threadfin or Thai mergui)
2 cloves garlic, chopped
2–3 dried red finger-length chillies,
   deseeded and broken into pieces, or
   1 teaspoon dried chilli flakes
350 g (7 cups) fresh bean sprouts, trimmed
2 teaspoons soy sauce
Vietnamese mint sprigs, to garnish

Bean sprouts with dried fish

Don't be fooled by the simplicity of this dish. Crispy-fried salt fish adds an appealing salty taste and aroma to the otherwise plain bean sprouts, and has made this dish a favourite among the Malaysians and Thais. It is a home-cooked dish, to be shared around the table with bowls of steaming hot rice. I remember we used to tuck in with chopsticks or forks, ladling some of the bean sprouts and that precious gravy, and searching for the last morsels of fish among the remains…which when found, how sublime! An aroma and taste I would climb Mount Fuji for!

Heat the oil in a wok until hot and fry the salted fish over medium heat for 2–3 minutes until crisp. Remove from the heat and drain on paper towels.

   Pour off all but 1 tablespoon of the oil in the wok. Reheat the oil and stir-fry the garlic and red chillies over high heat until golden and fragrant, about 30 seconds. Add the bean sprouts and toss well, about 1 minute. Stir in the fried fish and remove from the heat, then season with soy sauce. Transfer to a serving platter, garnish with Vietnamese mint sprigs and serve hot with steamed rice.

SERVES: *4*   PREPARATION TIME: *30 mins*   COOKING TIME: *5 mins*

300 g (10 oz) young okra, stems trimmed
1 teaspoon cornstarch
$\frac{1}{2}$ teaspoon ground turmeric
$\frac{1}{4}$ cup (60 ml) plain yoghurt
$\frac{1}{2}$ teaspoon ground red pepper

FILLING
5 tablespoons dried prawns, dry-roasted
    and crushed (see note)
1 tablespoon dried mango powder
    (*amchoor*), or $\frac{1}{2}$ teaspoon tamarind
    pulp mixed with as little water as
    possible to make a paste
1 tablespoon grated fresh ginger
2 tablespoons Sambal Oelek Chilli Paste
    (page 26), or Chilli Sambal (page 26)
1 tablespoon dried unsweetened grated
    (desiccated) coconut, dry-roasted in a
    pan until golden
1 teaspoon Dijon mustard
2 teaspoons sugar, or to taste
Pinch of salt, or to taste
3 teaspoons water

Okra stuffed with prawn sambal

Dry-roasted and cooked dried prawns take on an inviting fragrance of nutty fried fish. In this recipe, the aromatic addition of prawn stuffing with buttery roasted coconut and the spike of ginger transform the plain okra (or ladies' fingers), giving it life.

Prepare the Sambal Oelek Chilli Paste or Chilli Sambal by following the recipes on page 26.

Rinse the okra well, then drain and dry with paper towels. Make a slit along the side of each okra with a sharp knife, making sure not to cut through it and that the slit does not continue until the tip. Carefully remove the seeds and pith. Set aside. Combine all the Filling ingredients in a bowl and mix well. Stuff each okra by gently opening up the slit and filling it with 1 teaspoon of the Filling, using a fork or chopstick to press it in.

Preheat the oven to 160°C (325°F).

Mix the cornstarch and turmeric together on a plate. Roll each stuffed okra in the turmeric mixture to coat well, then place them on a baking sheet and bake in the oven for 20 minutes. Remove from the heat and arrange in a serving plate in a shallow yoghurt bath. Sprinkle with ground red pepper and and serve immediately.

Note: Dry-roast the dried prawns by placing them in a shallow dish and microwave on high for 2 minutes. Remove from the oven, stir well and return to microwave for 1 more minute until crisp. Grind or crush them by placing them between sheets of baking paper and roll them with a rolling pin, or pulse them quickly a few times in a blender or food processor.

SERVES: *4*   **PREPARATION TIME:** *30 mins*   **COOKING TIME:** *20 mins*

700 g (1½ lbs) slender Asian eggplants
2 teaspoons salt
½ tablespoon grated fresh turmeric root,
    or ½ teaspoon ground turmeric
1 cup (250 ml) light olive oil, for frying
30 g (¼ cup) raw cashew nuts, dry-roasted

SPICE PASTE
2 teaspoons cumin seeds, dry-roasted
1 teaspoon fennel seeds, dry-roasted
5 cm (2 in) fresh ginger, peeled and sliced
5 cloves garlic, peeled
2 stalks lemongrass, thick bottom part only,
    outer layers discarded, inner part sliced
2 onions, peeled and quartered
3 tablespoons extra virgin olive oil
2 tablespoons Fish Curry Powder (page 29)
1 tablespoon black mustard seeds, coarsely
    crushed in a mortar
2 teaspoons ground red pepper
½ cup (125 ml) white vinegar
2 tablespoon shaved palm sugar or dark
    brown sugar

SERVES: *6*

PREPARATION TIME: *45 mins*

COOKING TIME: *15 mins*

Delicious eggplant sambal with cashews

This aromatic sambal with an aroma of heady garlic, lime-like lemongrass and cumin has an additional layer of aromatic fennel and pungent mustard. The slow-cooking makes it possible for all the spice aromas to be separately enjoyed and the vinegar heightens the spice scents. This is a wonderful pickled sambal with exceptional fragrance and taste.

Prepare the Fish Curry Powder by following the recipe on page 29.

Cut the eggplants into 2.5 cm (1 in) thick slices. Combine the salt and grated turmeric in a small bowl and mix well. Brush the eggplant slices with the mixture and set aside for 10 minutes, then press between paper towels to dry.

Heat the olive oil in a skillet and in small batches, fry the eggplant slices over medium heat until light brown, 1–2 minutes on each side. Remove from the heat and drain on paper towels.

To prepare the Spice Paste, grind the cumin and fennel seeds in a spice grinder until fine. Combine with the ginger, garlic, lemongrass and onion, and grind to a smooth paste in a mortar or food processor. Heat the olive oil in a skillet and sauté the ground paste over medium heat until fragrant, 2–3 minutes. Add the Fish Curry Powder and continue to sauté for 1 more minute. Move the spice mixture to the sides of the pan, increase the heat to high, add the mustard seeds and cook until they begin to pop, then combine them with the spice mixture from the sides of the pan and mix well. Stir in the ground red pepper and season with the vinegar and sugar.

Add the cashew nuts and fried eggplant slices and toss until the eggplant is coated well with the sauce, taking care not to tear the pieces. Adjust the taste and remove from the heat. Serve hot or cold. This dish is especially tasty when served with baked ham, moussaka and crisp lettuce, or with steamed or fried fish.

Eggplant and tofu with sweet spicy bean paste

Eggplant and tofu are interesting and versatile ingredients. I use them in many of my dishes. Brown bean paste is similar to Japanese red miso—it has a nutty and smoky aroma, and when combined with oyster sauce and plum sauce, the result is an amazingly aromatic dish, which goes very well with rice.

$^3/_8$ cup (100 ml) oil

400 g (14 oz) slender Asian eggplants, thickly sliced diagonally

2 cakes pressed firm tofu (each 150 g/5 oz), cubed

2 cloves garlic, chopped

1–2 red finger-length chillies, deseeded and finely chopped

1 tablespoon brown bean paste (*taucheo*)

2 tablespoons oyster sauce

2 teaspoons bottled plum sauce

3 green onions (scallions), leaves sliced diagonally, to garnish

SERVES: *6*   PREPARATION TIME: *20 mins*
COOKING TIME: *20 mins*

Heat the oil in a wok until hot and fry the eggplant slices in batches over medium heat until golden, 2–3 minutes. Remove from the heat, drain on paper towels and keep warm until ready to use.

Drain off all but $^1/_4$ cup (60 ml) of the oil from the wok. Reheat the oil and shallow-fry the tofu cubes over medium heat until golden and crisp on all sides in the same manner. Remove from the heat and drain on paper towels.

Clean the wok, heat 2 teaspoons of the oil in it and stir-fry the garlic, chilli and bean paste over medium heat until fragrant, about 1 minute. Stir in the fried eggplant pieces, the oyster sauce and the plum sauce. Add the fried tofu and toss quickly to combine, then remove from the heat. Transfer to a serving platter, garnish with the green onion and serve hot with steamed rice.

Asian greens with prawns and cashews

Chinese broccoli (*kailan*) and other dark Asian greens have a slightly bitter taste that translates also to a "bitter" aroma. When combined with garlic and the delicious buttery perfume of sautéed prawns, this dish swells with fragrance, especially when mushrooms and cashew nuts are added.

1 tablespoon oil

2 cloves garlic, minced

12 fresh prawns, peeled and deveined

12 dried black Chinese mushrooms, soaked in hot water until soft, stems trimmed, caps sliced

1 teaspoon Sambal Oelek chilli paste (page 26) or other sweet chilli paste

1 bunch Chinese broccoli (*kailan*), stems only, peeled and sliced diagonally

200 g (2 cups) sliced bok choy

2 tablespoons oyster sauce

$^1/_2$ teaspoon sesame oil

Salt and ground white pepper, to taste

Dry-roasted cashew nuts, to garnish

Crispy Fried Garlic (page 30), to garnish

Prepare the Sambal Oelek Chilli Paste and Crispy Fried Garlic by following the recipes on pages 26 and 30.

Heat the oil in a wok and stir-fry the garlic over medium heat until fragrant and golden, about 1 minute. Add the prawns, mushroom slices and Sambal Oelek and stir-fry for 1 minute. Add the vegetables and toss well over high heat for 2 minutes until tender. Season with the oyster sauce, sesame oil, salt and pepper to taste, and remove from the heat. Transfer to a serving platter, sprinkle with cashew nuts and Crispy Fried Garlic on top and serve hot with steamed rice.

Note: To prepare as a vegetarian dish, simply omit the prawns.

SERVES: *4*   PREPARATION TIME: *20 mins*   COOKING TIME: *5 mins*

VEGETABLE DISHES

desserts and drinks

Black rice pudding with ginger coconut cream

Black sticky rice is unusually dark purple in colour. I am often asked if it has been coloured. It is indeed natural, coming with its own pandanus-like grassy fresh perfume with a hint of coconut in the top notes that is reinforced by adding coconut cream as a final swirl in this dessert. Black sticky rice has a ready following whenever it is served as it engages the instincts with its contrasting colours, textures and subtle scents.

100 g ($^1/_2$ cup) uncooked black
   sticky (glutinous) rice, washed
4 cups (1 litre) water
1 fresh pandanus leaf, cut into long
   strips and then tied into knots,
   or 2–3 drops pandanus essence
12 mm ($^1/_2$ in) fresh ginger, thinly sliced
150 g ($^3/_4$ cup) sugar
Salt, to taste
Coconut cream, to serve

In a saucepan, bring the rice, water, pandanus leaf or essence and ginger to a boil. Reduce the heat to a simmer and cook the mixture uncovered for about 30 minutes until the grains are soft, adding more water as necessary.

Add the sugar and stir until it is dissolved. Season with salt to taste and remove from the heat. Ladle into serving bowls and serve hot or chilled with a drizzle of coconut cream on top.

SERVES: *4*   PREPARATION TIME: *5 mins*   COOKING TIME: *30 mins*

Green mango and saffron lassi shakes

A lassi is a refreshingly tangy drink made with yoghurt. This one, made with green mangoes, is different. Although lacking the ripe pineapple-honey mango aromas, it is fragrant with the luxurious honeysuckle of unripe mango and saffron reminiscent of Middle Eastern souks—one can imagine drinking this in gilded tents surrounded by rich treasures, served by a genie in a bottle.

2 unripe green mangoes (about 350 g/
   12 oz total), peeled, pitted and diced
2 cups (500 ml) water
100 g ($^1/_2$ cup) sugar
Salt, to taste
2 cups (500 ml) chilled milk
8–10 saffron threads, soaked in 2 tablespoons
   warm milk for 30 minutes, plus
   additional saffron threads, to garnish

MAKES: *4 glasses*

PREPARATION TIME: *10 mins + 4 hours*
   to chill

COOKING TIME: *5 mins*

In a saucepan, bring the mango pieces and water to a simmer and cook over medium heat until the mango pulp softens, 2–3 minutes. Add the sugar and stir until the sugar dissolves. Remove from the heat and process the mango mixture to a purée in a food processor. Strain the purée into a jug and stir in the salt to taste, then chill in the refrigerator for at least 4 hours.

To serve, process the chilled milk, saffron milk mixture and chilled mango purée until well blended. Pour into individual serving glasses and garnish each one with a saffron thread.

Note: If you find the green mangoes too tart, adjust the taste by adding more sugar to the purée.

DESSERTS AND DRINKS

1/2 cup (125 ml) coconut cream
230 g (1 cup) butter
100 g (1/2 cup) fine granulated sugar
100 g (1/2 cup) shaved palm sugar or dark
   brown sugar
5 eggs
250 g (2 cups) self-raising flour, sifted three
   times with a pinch of salt.
75 g (3/4 cup) freshly grated coconut,
   dry-roasted over low heat for 10 minutes

PANDANUS JUICE
5 pandanus leaves, rinsed and sliced
1 tablespoon water

PALM SUGAR SYRUP
200 g (1 cup) shaved palm sugar
1 1/4 cups (300 ml) water

Pandanus coconut cake with palm sugar syrup

This is essentially a buttercake recipe, with fresh pandanus juice substituted for vanilla, enriched with coconut cream and grated coconut. You will enjoy this enticingly moist cake with its delicate grassy and floral aromas reminiscent of waving palms and sandy beaches.

Make the Pandanus Juice first by grinding the sliced pandanus leaves in a mortar or blender until fine, adding the water gradually. Wrap the mixture in a muslin cloth and squeeze out the juice, or use a very fine sieve. Add the juice to the coconut cream and mix well.

Preheat the oven to 170°C (340°F). Cream the butter and sugars with an electric mixer until smooth. With the motor running, add the eggs, one at a time, and mix well after each addition. Fold in the flour and coconut cream alternately with a spatula or wooden spoon, and mix until well blended, then fold in the grated coconut. Spoon the mixture into a greased round cake pan, smooth the top and bake in the oven, on the middle shelf, for 40 minutes. The cake is ready when it pulls away from the sides of the cake pan. Remove from the oven and set aside to cool, then turn out onto a serving plate.

While the cake is baking, prepare the Palm Sugar Syrup by combining the palm sugar and water in a heatproof dish. Microwave the mixture for 1 minute on high, then remove and stir. Repeat to cook for 2 more minutes in the same manner until all the sugar is dissolved.

To serve, drizzle the Palm Sugar Syrup over the cake or over each portion.

MAKES: *1*   **PREPARATION TIME:** *30 mins*   **COOKING TIME:** *40 mins*

Semolina halva with almonds

With each step of this recipe, we are creating aromas. The dry-roasted semolina comes first, followed by a caramelised syrup and finally the sweetish cardamom is added to give this fragrant dessert the scent of Persian cuisine.

1 cup (250 ml) milk
1 cup (250 ml) water
1 teaspoon cardamom seeds, lightly
 crushed
150 g ($^3/_4$ cup) sugar
125 g ($^1/_2$ cup) butter
185 g (1 cup) large-grain semolina
50 g ($^1/_4$ cup) raisins
2 tablespoons raw sliced almonds, dry-
 roasted
$^1/_4$ cup (60 ml) golden syrup (optional)

SERVES: *6–8*
PREPARATION TIME: *40 mins*

Bring the milk, water and cardamom to a boil in a saucepan. Remove from the heat, add the sugar and stir until the sugar is dissolved. Set aside and allow to cool slightly.

In a wok, melt the butter over medium heat and stir-fry the semolina until golden brown and fragrant. Do not allow the wok to get too hot or the semolina will burn. Add the raisins and stir-fry for another 1 minute. Reduce the heat to low, pour in the milk mixture and simmer for 4–5 minutes, stirring quickly, until the liquid has reduced. Remove from the heat.

Pour the cooked mixture into a buttered 20-cm (8-in) pie plate. Smooth the surface with the back of a buttered spoon and slice into diamond shapes using a knife or cookie cutter. Arrange on a serving platter and decorate each piece with the almond slices. Drizzle with the golden syrup (if using) and serve warm or cold with coffee.

Note: This dish keeps for a week in the refrigerator wrapped in plastic wrap. Before serving, bring refrigerated halva to room temperature or warm gently in a microwave or an oven.

Spiced mangoes in yoghurt and honey

The heady "honey and peaches" aroma of ripe mangoes blend naturally with a smooth natural yoghurt base. This dessert is enticingly garnished with drizzled honey and the subtle aromas of sprinkled golden saffron threads. A hint of cardamom ties the dish together as it strengthens the yoghurt.

1 cup (250 ml) thick plain yoghurt
2 cardamom pods, skins removed and
 seeds ground to a powder, or 1 teaspoon
 ground cardamom
2 tablespoons honey
1 tablespoon golden syrup
2 ripe mangoes, peeled, pitted and thinly
 sliced into sheaths
Warm honey, to serve
Few strands of saffron, soaked in 1 teaspoon
 yoghurt, to garnish

In a mixing bowl, combine the yoghurt, ground cardamom, honey and golden syrup and whip until well blended.

To serve, spoon the whipped yoghurt mixture into serving bowls and lay 2 mango sheaths on top, then drizzle with some warm honey over them and garnish with the saffron strands.

SERVES: *4*   PREPARATION TIME: *15 mins*

Sweet coconut custard

Another coconut custard with spicy cardamom and the sweet aroma of pandanus or vanilla and ginger. It is interesting to note how a few spices can change the whole flavour of a humble custard.

60 g (¹/₃ cup) shaved palm sugar or dark brown sugar

2 cardamom pods, lightly smash, seeds removed and ground in a mortar to a powder or ¹/₂ teaspoon ground cardamom

2 tablespoons water

7 egg yolks

1 cup (250 ml) thick coconut milk

2 pandanus leaves, each tied into a knot, or 1 vanilla bean, split

1¹/₂ cups (375 ml) coconut cream

4 tablespoons candied ginger, thinly sliced

Grated rind of 1 lime

1 tablespoon fresh lime juice

2 teaspoons rum plus 2 tablespoons rum for syrup

6 oven-proof bowls (each holding about 1 cup/250 ml)

PANDANUS SYRUP

3 cups (750 ml) water

300 g (1¹/₂ cups) sugar

1 pandanus leaf, tied into a knot, or 2–3 drops pandanus essence

SERVES: *6*

PREPARATION TIME: *10-15 mins*

COOKING TIME: *45 mins*

Prepare the Pandanus Syrup first by heating all the ingredients in a saucepan over medium heat and stirring until the sugar is dissolved. Bring to a boil, then simmer uncovered for about 30 seconds and remove from the heat. Discard the pandanus leaf and set the syrup aside to cool.

Preheat the oven to 170°C (340°F).

In a small saucepan, heat the sugar, cardamom and water over medium heat, stirring until the sugar is dissolved. Remove from the heat and set aside to cool. Transfer to a bowl, add the egg yolks and coconut milk, and beat until light and fluffy. Add 1 pandanus leaf or the split vanilla bean to the mixture.

Place the coconut cream, the other pandanus leaf and the ginger in the top of a double boiler and heat gently over medium heat. Gradually pour in the egg mixture but do not allow the mixture to boil. Cook over low heat for about 5 minutes then remove from the heat when the coconut mixture begins to simmer. Discard the pandanus leaves or vanilla bean, stir in ¹/₂ of the grated lime rind, the lime juice and rum, and mix well.

Pour the mixture into 6 oven-proof bowls and arrange in a baking dish. Half-fill the dish with boiling water and bake in the oven for about 40 minutes or until the custard is firm and the top has browned. Remove from the heat and top the custard with the remaining grated lime rind. Serve warm or chilled, drizzled with 1 tablespoon Pandanus Syrup or warmed maple syrup with 2 tablespoons rum added.

Note: If you prefer to caramelise the top of the custard, omit the lime rind garnish. Sprinkle ¹/₂ teaspoon of powdered sugar over the top of the custard and place the custard under a hot broiler grill until golden and crisp. Watch carefully as the sugar burns quickly.

8 ripe baby bananas or 4 ripe regular
   bananas, peeled
$^1/_2$ cup (125 ml) low fat fresh milk
1 tablespoon butter
2 tablespoons fresh lime juice
100 g ($^3/_4$ cup) self-raising flour, sifted
4 tablespoons rice flour, sifted
$^1/_2$ teaspoon ground cinnamon
$^1/_4$ cup (60 ml) oil, for frying

SUGAR SYRUP
100 g ($^1/_2$ cup) sugar
$^1/_4$ cup (60 ml) water
$^1/_2$ teaspoon ginger juice (optional)

Isaac's baby banana cinnamon pancakes

Bananas make surprisingly tasty tiny pancakes or pikelets, which can be prepared beforehand as the lime juice keeps them from darkening. The aroma of bananas and butter cooking makes the whole family salivate and makes up for the lack of sophistication in this simple dish—a favourite of my grandson Isaac, a six-year-old cook in his own right.

Prepare the Sugar Syrup first by bringing the ingredients to a boil in a small saucepan and stirring until the sugar is dissolved. Remove from the heat and set aside to cool. This makes about $^1/_2$ cup (125 ml) of Sugar Syrup. Alternatively, microwave the mixture for 3 minutes on medium, remove and stir until the sugar is dissolved, then return to microwave for 1 more minute.

    Process the bananas, milk, butter and lime juice in a food processor until smooth, then add the flours and continue processing to a smooth batter. Stir in the ground cinnamon and set aside for at least 1 hour.

    Heat the oil in a skillet until hot. Spoon 1 tablespoon of the batter into the hot oil, at the same time turning the skillet to form the batter into a thin round pancake. Fry the pancake over medium heat for 1–2 minutes until it begins to brown, then turn over and fry the other side for 30 seconds. Remove from the heat and drain on paper towels. Repeat to fry the remaining batter in the same manner. Serve the pancakes hot with the Sugar Syrup on the side.

SERVES: *4–6*   **PREPARATION TIME:** *15 mins*   **COOKING TIME:** *20 mins*

Planter's punch

The agostura aromas of anise and cinnamon contrast with lime, a heady sugar-hit of rum and the rose-like grenadine give you an exotic, zesty and refreshing drink to enjoy at sundown with good company. This was served with lime slices in English social clubs throughout the colonial empire. Planters punch provides a more sophisticated tropical alternative to beer.

1¹/₂ oz (45 ml) dark rum
1¹/₂ oz (45 ml) fresh lime juice
Few drops angostura bitters
1 oz (30 ml) grenadine syrup
3 cups (750 ml) chilled soda water
4 swizzle sticks
Grated lime rind, to garnish
Crushed ice or ice cubes, to serve
4 chilled glasses

Pour the ingredients into a 1.5–2 litres pitcher, one on top of another, in the sequence as listed in the ingredient list. After the addition of chilled soda water at the end, stir the layers of ingredients with a swizzle stick. Pour into 4 chilled glasses and serve immediately garnished with grated lime and crushed ice.

SERVES: *4*   PREPARATION TIME: *20 mins*

Pineapple, starfruit and carrot coolers

This is a healthy and quick pick-me-up, especially if you have a juicer. The chilli and ginger add a peppery aroma and bite to the ripe, floral notes of the pineapple. I would recommend this drink on a winter's morning or when you feel a cold coming on.

350 g (2 cups) fresh ripe pineapple slices
1 large starfruit or 2 green apples, sliced
1 carrot, peeled and sliced
1 tablespoon fresh lime juice
2 tablespoons honey
2 drops Tabasco sauce or ¹/₂ teaspoon
    fresh ginger juice
4 thin slices of starfruit, to garnish

Chill the fruit and carrot, then juice separately in a juicer. Combine all the juices in a pitcher, add the lime juice and honey, and mix until well blended. Stir in the Tabasco sauce or ginger juice with a swizzle stick. Pour into individual glasses, garnish with the starfruit slices and serve at once.

SERVES: *4*   PREPARATION TIME: *15 mins*

Pineapple gin slings

The iconic gin sling, famous for its combination of fragrant aromas and flavours, has been enjoyed for over a century at the Raffles Hotel in Singapore. The sweet cherry brandy on top of zesty lime juice and aromatic pineapple, topped with the anise of angostura and cinnamon of Benedictine all contained in one drink—surely a piece of heaven in a glass!

8 oz (250 ml) gin
4 oz (125 ml) cherry brandy
2 oz (60 ml) fresh lime juice
4 cups (1 litre) unsweetened fresh or
    canned pineapple juice
3 oz (100 ml) grenadine syrup
3 dashes Benedictine Dom
Dash of triple sec
Few drops of angostura bitters
3 slices lime, halved, to garnish
Mint leaves, to garnish
6 swizzle sticks

Fill a large chilled pitcher a quarter full with ice cubes. Pour in all the ingredients, one by one, and stir the mixture twice. Strain the drink into 6 highball glasses filled with ice cubes. Garnish each glass with a half a slice of lime and serve with a mint leaf and swizzle stick.

MAKES: *6 glasses*   PREPARATION TIME: *45 mins*

Pandanus lemonade

Citrusy lemonade dressed up for the tropics with the grassy perfume of fresh pandanus—if you are adventurous, add a few slices of nose tingling ginger to the syrup. Serve this chilled on a hot summer evening. Pandanus and ginger lift the lemonade giving it a suggestion of a bite.

1 cup (250 ml) fresh lemon juice
1 cup (250 ml) fresh lime juice
8 cups (2 litres) iced water
Crushed ice
Grated lime rind, to garnish
Sprigs of mint leaves, to garnish

PANDANUS SUGAR SYRUP
2 pandanus leaves, tied into a knot
200 g (1 cup) sugar
$^1/_2$ cup (125 ml) water

Prepare the Pandanus Sugar Syrup by bringing the ingredients to a boil in a saucepan and stirring until the sugar is dissolved. Remove from the heat and cool.

Combine the cooled Pandanus Sugar Syrup with the lemon juice, lime juice and iced water in a pitcher and stir well, then chill in the refrigerator until ready to serve.

To serve, pour into individual serving glasses filled with crushed ice, top with grated lime rind and garnish with mint leaves.

Note: A tablespoon of vodka or gin may be added to create a light cocktail.

MAKES: *6-8 glasses*   PREPARATION TIME: *15 mins*
COOKING TIME: *5 mins*

DESSERTS AND DRINKS

INDEX

ACKNOWLEDGEMENTS

This book has been slow-cooking for a long time like any good dish, with spice and herb. Starting as a book on the aromatics of Malaysian food, it contained traditional recipes with a working title we called "Ginger Flower."

My daughter Anushiya Selvarajah, a trained teacher of Asian cooking for over 10 years, assisted by Patricia Soosay from Perth, who wanted to gain more of an understanding of Malaysian cooking, tested recipes for months. Both girls knew the food and understood the cuisine just as much as I did, yet we found ourselves re-testing, changing and sometimes reverting to our original recipes in an attempt to improve and to simplify techniques. Finally without any murders or mayhem, the recipes were collated and I thank both Patricia and Anushiya sincerely for teasing out the best flavours with dedication and care.

Thanks also go to Matt Lim and to Diane Temple for her careful recipe formatting. The help and friendship of Philippa Sandall, Andrea Rademan and Wendy Lloyd Jones have, as always, been invaluable.

I include some recipes from friends whose work I admire: Lyndey Milan and Di Holuigue, Pauline Loh, Patricia Soosay, Simon Goh and Marty Morrison. I would also like to thank Michelle Sandhu, my niece in Singapore, my brother Abel Arumugam and his wife Gomathy, and Andrea Rademan in Beverly Hills, California, for the use of their kitchens and their computers while working abroad and for their generosity, to Christina Ong for her creative eye and food-styling that has guided the book's tone and atmosphere and to Masano for his photography. Thanks also to Dr. Max Lake, OAM.FRCS, International wine judge and author of six books on flavour, taste and aroma. I would not have dared to venture into this realm had I not been convinced of Max's support and critique; to dear friends Cheong Liew for his support and David Thompson for writing the foreword.

And to Ben Cardillo, for allowing me to see my Malaysia through his eyes, when, in 1991, he wished we had smell-a-vision while we were filming for a television series in Kuala Lumpur. The following books were used as references:

Spice Notes by Ian Hemphill
Dictionary of Japanese Foods by Richard Hosking
The Chinese Kitchen by Deh-Ta Hsuing
Thai Food by David Thompson
Taste by Max Lake
Sense and Sensuality by Max Lake
Tropical Planting and Gardening by H.E. Holtum and Macmillan, revised by Barlow Enoch and Russel

DEDICATION

Aromas have seldom been explored for themselves except by vintners, sommeliers and perfumers, although they are recognised as an integral part of flavour. A Malaysian housewife prides herself on food that is *wangi* or *ho heong*, as my Amah used to say. Aromas intrigue when they are combined carefully into a fragrance that is difficult to analyse and yet at the edge of your senses, as they bypass the cognitive brain, going directly to the emotive. So enjoy aromas in food by breathing deeply and sitting down to eat, as you use all your senses for a complete experience.

To my family and many friends who have perfumed my life, this book is for you—with love.

Published by Tuttle Publishing, an imprint of Periplus Editions (HK) Ltd., with editorial offices at 364 Innovation Drive, North Clarendon, Vermont 05759 USA and 61 Tai Seng Avenue, #02-12, Singapore 534167

Text and recipes © 2009 Carol Selva Rajah
Photos copyright © 2009 Periplus Editions
All rights reserved.

ISBN: 978-0-8048-4125-2
(Previously published as Heavenly Fragrance)

Distributed by
North America, Latin America & Europe
Tuttle Publishing
364 Innovation Drive
North Clarendon, VT 05759-9436 U.S.A.
Tel: 1 (802) 773-8930; Fax: 1 (802) 773-6993
info@tuttlepublishing.com
www.tuttlepublishing.com

Japan
Tuttle Publishing
Yaekari Building, 3rd Floor
5-4-12 Osaki, Shinagawa-ku
Tokyo 141 0032
Tel: (81) 03 5437-0171; Fax: (81) 03 5437-0755
tuttle-sales@gol.com

Asia Pacific
Berkeley Books Pte. Ltd.
61 Tai Seng Avenue, #02-12
Singapore 534167
Tel: (65) 6280-1330; Fax: (65) 6280-6290
inquiries@periplus.com.sg
www.periplus.com

All recipes were tested in the Periplus Test Kitchen.

Photo credits: All photography by Masano Kawana except pages 6; 8–11. Drawing representation of author's home taken from old photographs and created by Carolyn McCulloch, Sydney. Page 11: Market photograph, Ray Williams Photography, Sydney. Backflap photograph (author's photo): Ronald Leong Singapore.

Design by the Periplus design team

Printed in Malaysia
12 11 10 09   6 5 4 3 2 1

TUTTLE PUBLISHING® is a registered trademark of Tuttle Publishing, a division of Periplus Editions (HK) Ltd.